Bible FUNSTUFF

Folder Games

FOR CHILDREN'S MINISTRY

EDITED BY
Susan Martins Miller

© 2003 Cook Communications Ministries

All rights reserved. No part of this book may be reproduced without written permission, except for brief quotations in books and critical reviews. For information, write Cook Communications Ministries, 4050 Lee Vance View, Colorado Springs, Colorado 80918.

First printing 2002

1 2 3 4 5 6 7 8 9 10   08 07 06 05 04 03

Printed in the United States of America

Written by Mary Grace Becker, Lois Keffer, Susan Martins Miller and Dawn Renee Weary

Cover Design by Peter Schmidt and Scot McDonald, Granite Design

Interior Design by Dana Sherrer, iDesignEtc.

Unless otherwise noted, Scripture quotations are taken from THE HOLY BIBLE NEW INTERNATIONAL VERSION (NIV), Copyright © 1973, 1978, 1984 by International Bible Society. Used by permission of Zondervan Publishing House. All rights reserved.

ISBN: 0781439612

Table of Contents

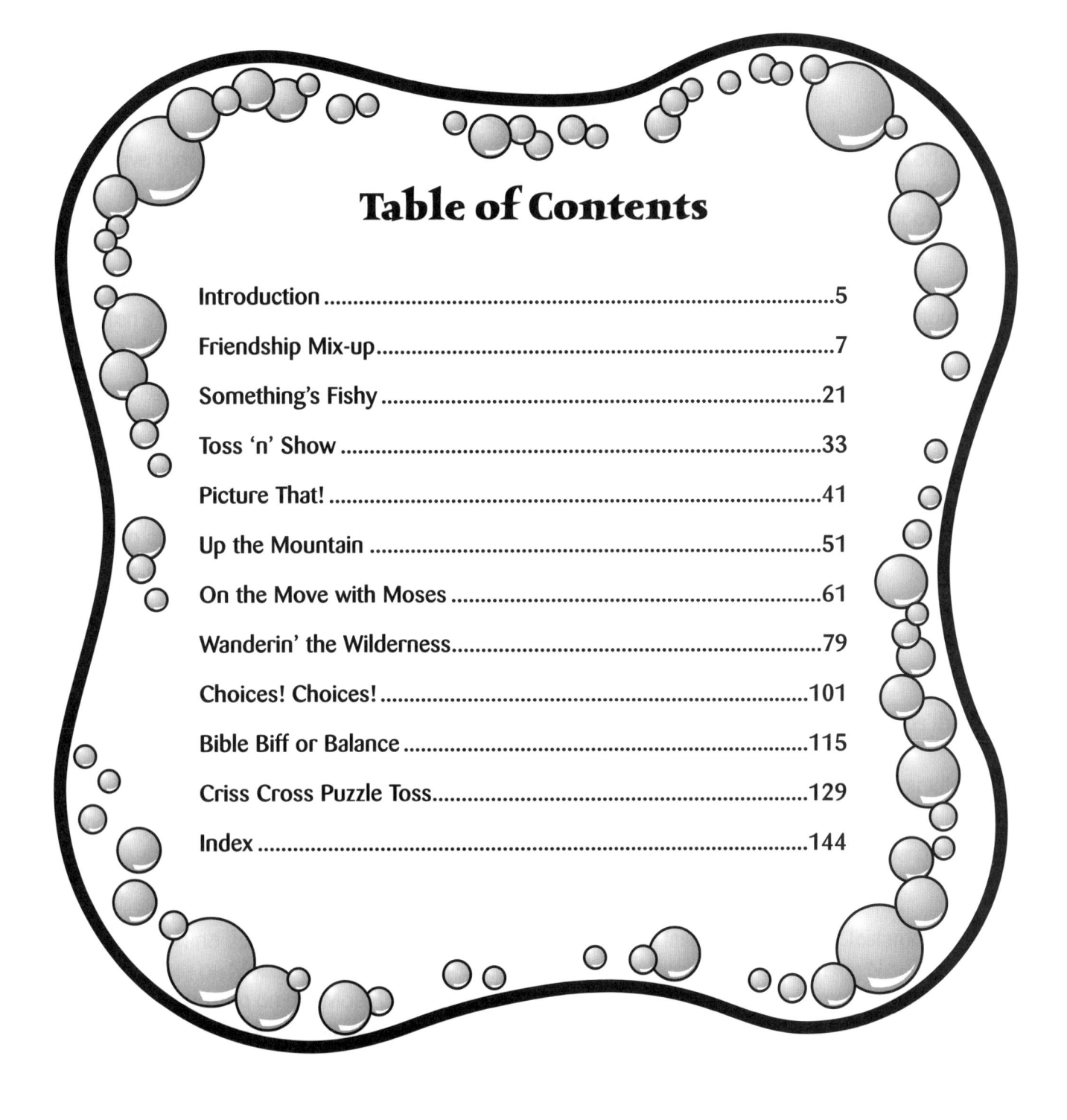

Introduction 5

Friendship Mix-up 7

Something's Fishy 21

Toss 'n' Show 33

Picture That! 41

Up the Mountain 51

On the Move with Moses 61

Wanderin' the Wilderness 79

Choices! Choices! 101

Bible Biff or Balance 115

Criss Cross Puzzle Toss 129

Index 144

2. Glue the colored pages onto the panels of a colorful file folder. Glue the game title to the front of the folder. Glue "How to Play" to the back. Glue the gameboard panels inside the folder.

3. For added durability, laminate the finished game folders, cards and spinners. If you can't laminate, try covering game folders with clear self-adhesive paper, such as Contact® paper. Trim away the excess.

4. Cover a cardboard box or plastic crate with colorful wrapping paper. Use the box or crate to store your games so they're always ready when you need them.

So get ready to fold, cut and glue your way to a richer children's ministry—helping children experience the touch of God on their lives as they grow into mature disciples.

Here's everything you need to make all the games in this book.

Brads
Buttons
Colored markers or pencils
Coins (nickels, pennies, quarters)
Dry beans
Envelopes
File folders in bright colors
Glue
Hole punch
Index cards in bright colors
Paper clips (large, colorful)
Pencils
Plastic cups (9-oz. clear)
Scissors
Scrap paper
Tape (clear)
Timer
Wagon wheel pasta
Yarn
Zip-top bags

Friendship Mix-Up

The Bible is full of friendships with valuable lessons. How many can you identify?

Godprint: Friendliness

Players: 2 to 4 players or teams

Put It Together

1. Add color to the gameboard and clue cards as you wish.

2. Cut out the game title (above) and glue it to the front of the folder.

3. Glue "How to Play" (page 9) to the back of the folder. Leave space above the rules to glue an envelope or zip-top bag to the folder.

4. Glue page 12 to the left inside of the folder. Glue page 13 to the right inside of the folder.

5. Cut apart the clue cards on pages 15, 17 and 19.

6. Store the clue cards in the envelope or zip-top bag.

7. Laminate as desired.

GET LIST:
- envelope or zip-top bag
- scissors
- glue
- colored pencils or markers

Glue to the front of the game folder.

How to Play

1. Find out how to honor God through friendship by remembering favorite Bible stories about friends. The goal of this game is to collect the letters that spell "FRIEND." You can play with two to four players or with teams. You can collect the letters in any order.

2. Sort the clue cards according to the letters on the back. Put the clue cards on the matching letters on the gameboard. Make sure the question side faces down.

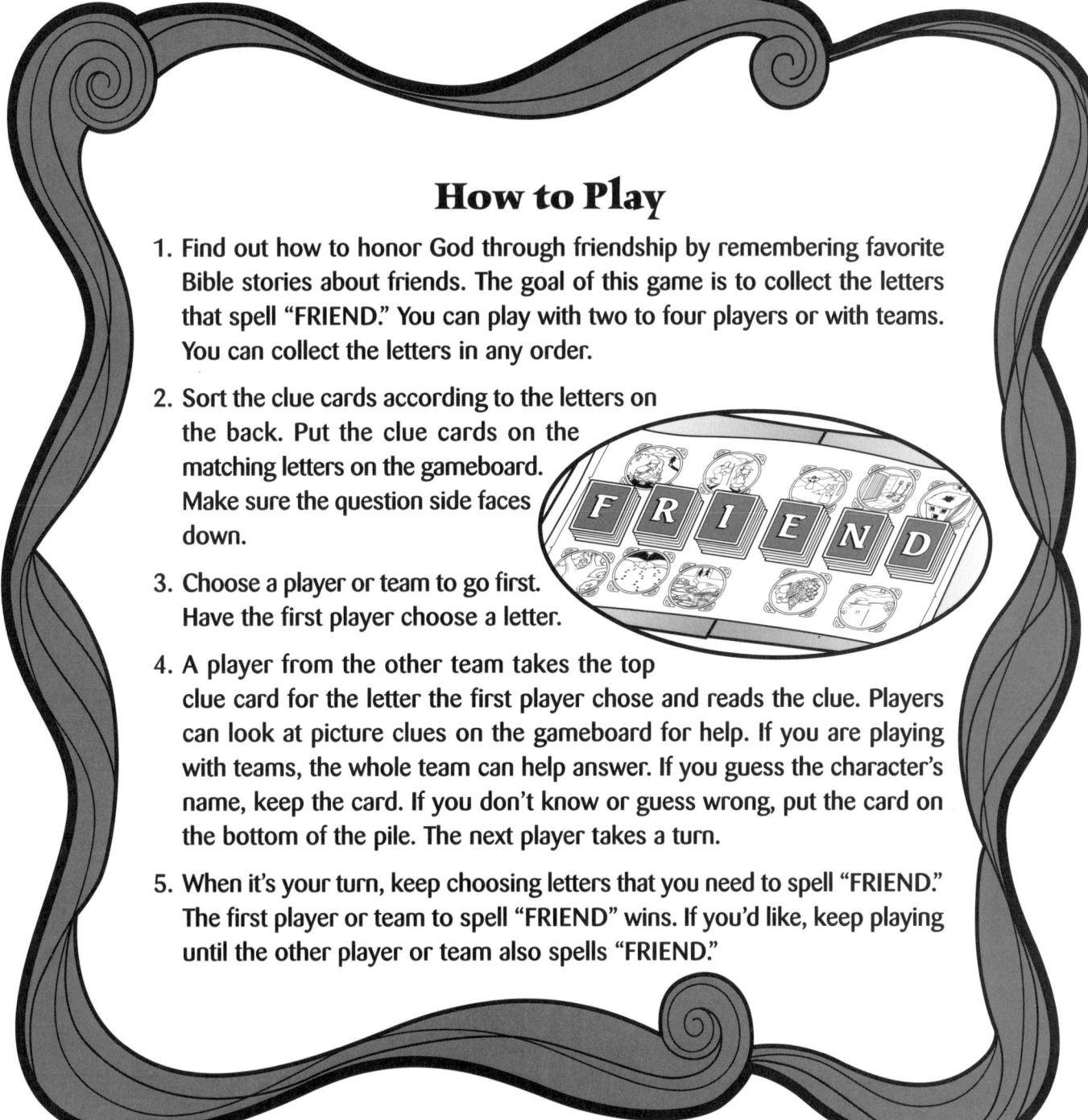

3. Choose a player or team to go first. Have the first player choose a letter.

4. A player from the other team takes the top clue card for the letter the first player chose and reads the clue. Players can look at picture clues on the gameboard for help. If you are playing with teams, the whole team can help answer. If you guess the character's name, keep the card. If you don't know or guess wrong, put the card on the bottom of the pile. The next player takes a turn.

5. When it's your turn, keep choosing letters that you need to spell "FRIEND." The first player or team to spell "FRIEND" wins. If you'd like, keep playing until the other player or team also spells "FRIEND."

Cut out these playing rules and glue them to the back of the game folder.

friendship mix-up

F R I

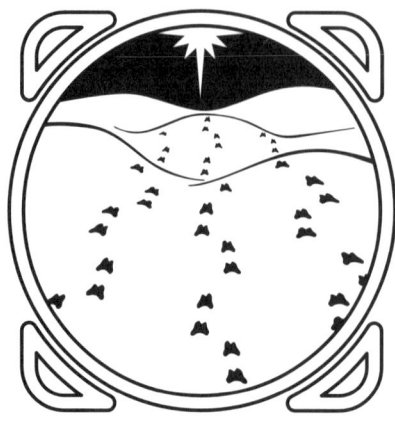

E N D

Glue inside the right side of the game folder.

My best friend was a prince of a guy in a time of royal danger. Who am I? (David)	My friend's father, the king, wanted to kill me, but I knew my friend would help. Who am I? (David)	My friend would have been the next king, but he was happy that God had chosen me. Who am I? (David)	Even though I was a prince, I knew my best friend would make a great leader. Who am I? (Jonathan)
I kept my friend safe from his enemy—my father, the king! Who am I? (Jonathan)	My friend knew he could count on me to help him escape my father the king's anger. Who am I? (Jonathan)	My friend was my mother-in-law. Who am I? (Ruth)	I stayed with my mother-in-law because I did not want her to be alone. Who am I? (Ruth)
I worked in the field to help my friend have enough food to eat. Who am I? (Ruth)	My friend was my daughter-in-law. Who am I? (Naomi)	I was glad to have my daughter-in-law friend with me when I traveled from Moab to Bethlehem. Who am I? (Naomi)	My friend loved me so much she wanted to go wherever I went, even to a strange land. Who am I? (Naomi)
I was a little tax collector everyone looked down on, but when Jesus came, he looked up at me. Who am I? (Zacchaeus)	I didn't think Jesus wanted to be my friend when I climbed a tree to see him. Who am I? (Zacchaeus)	My new friend Jesus called me down from a tree because he wanted to go to my house! Who am I? (Zacchaeus)	I made friends with someone who had no friends and climbed a tree to see me. Who am I? (Jesus)

friendship mix-up

R	F	D	N
D	N	E	I
E	I	R	F
R	F	D	N

folder games

My four friends took me to see Jesus. Who am I? (Paralyzed man)	We wanted our friend to see Jesus, but the house was too crowded. Who are we? (Four friends of paralyzed man)	We took off part of the roof so our hurt friend could see Jesus. Who are we? (Four friends of paralyzed man)	We knew Jesus could help our friend pick up his mat and walk. Who are we? (Four friends of paralyzed man)
We friends made a long journey from the East to see a new king we knew would change the world. Who are we? (Wise men)	We friends stuck together to worship baby Jesus with our best gifts. Who are we? (Wise men)	We knew that Herod was no real friend of ours. We are we? (Wise men)	When I found out I was going to have a baby, I could hardly wait to tell my friend and relative, Elizabeth. Who am I? (Mary)
I was so glad my friend Elizabeth shared my joy about the baby I was going to have. Who am I? (Mary)	Sometimes a relative can be your best friend, like my friend Elizabeth. Who am I? (Mary)	We spoke up together for what God wanted when 10 other men were afraid of the giants. Who are we? (Caleb and Joshua)	While we spied out the promised land, we helped each other have faith that God would give us the land. Who are we? (Caleb and Joshua)
We went on a secret mission together for God with 10 other spies. Who are we? (Caleb and Joshua)	We could have had a big fight over land and water, but we worked things out as friends. Who are we? (Abraham and Lot)	Our servants wanted to fight about water for the flocks, but we didn't. Who are we? (Abraham and Lot)	We chose peace instead of arguing about land and water. Who are we? (Abraham and Lot)

friendship mix-up

D	N	E	I
E	I	R	F
R	F	D	N
D	N	E	I

folder games

Godprint: Repentance
Players: 2-6

Jonah learned about repentance the hard way! Follow his story and find out how you can turn away from selfishness and move toward God.

Put It Together

1. Add color to the gameboard and "Repent!" cards as you wish.

2. Cut out the game title (above) and glue it to the front of the game folder.

3. Glue "How to Play" (page 23) to the back of the folder. Leave space above the rules to glue a zip-top bag to hold the "Repent!" cards, game cube and paper clip playing pieces.

4. Glue page 26 to the left inside and page 27 to the right inside of the game folder.

Optional: Cut a piece of lightweight blue cellophane and cover the "sea" section of the gameboard, including the fish. Tape down securely around the edges.

5. Bend up the smaller inner loop of a large paper clip to make the sail for each playing piece "boat."

6. Laminate as desired.

GET LIST:
- game cube with numbers or dots, 1-6
- 6 large colorful paper clips
- glue
- scissors
- colored pencils or markers

something's fishy

Glue playing rules to the back of the game folder.

Glue inside the left side of the game folder.

something's fishy

Glue to the right inside of the game folder.

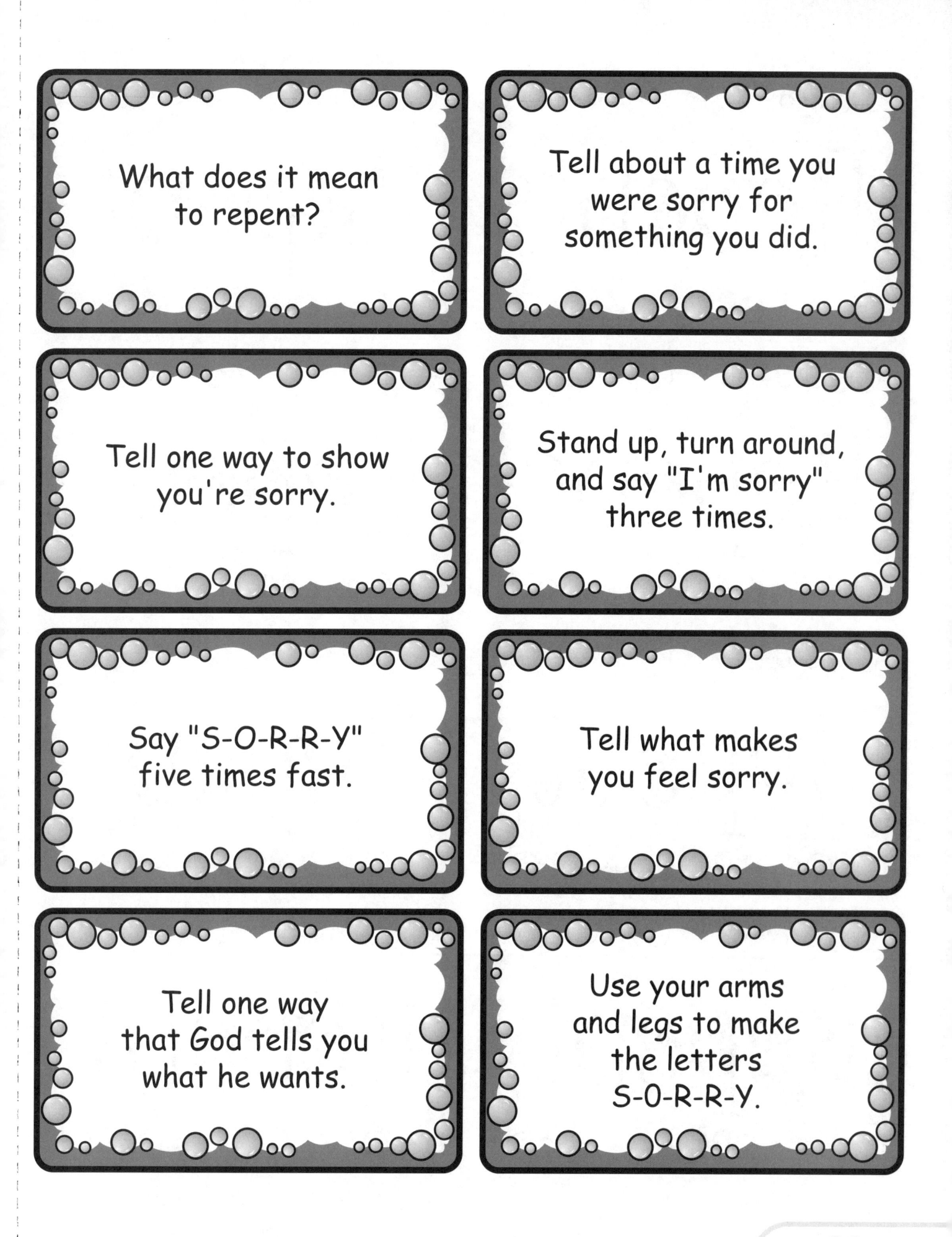

What does it mean to repent?	Tell about a time you were sorry for something you did.
Tell one way to show you're sorry.	Stand up, turn around, and say "I'm sorry" three times.
Say "S-O-R-R-Y" five times fast.	Tell what makes you feel sorry.
Tell one way that God tells you what he wants.	Use your arms and legs to make the letters S-O-R-R-Y.

something's fishy 29

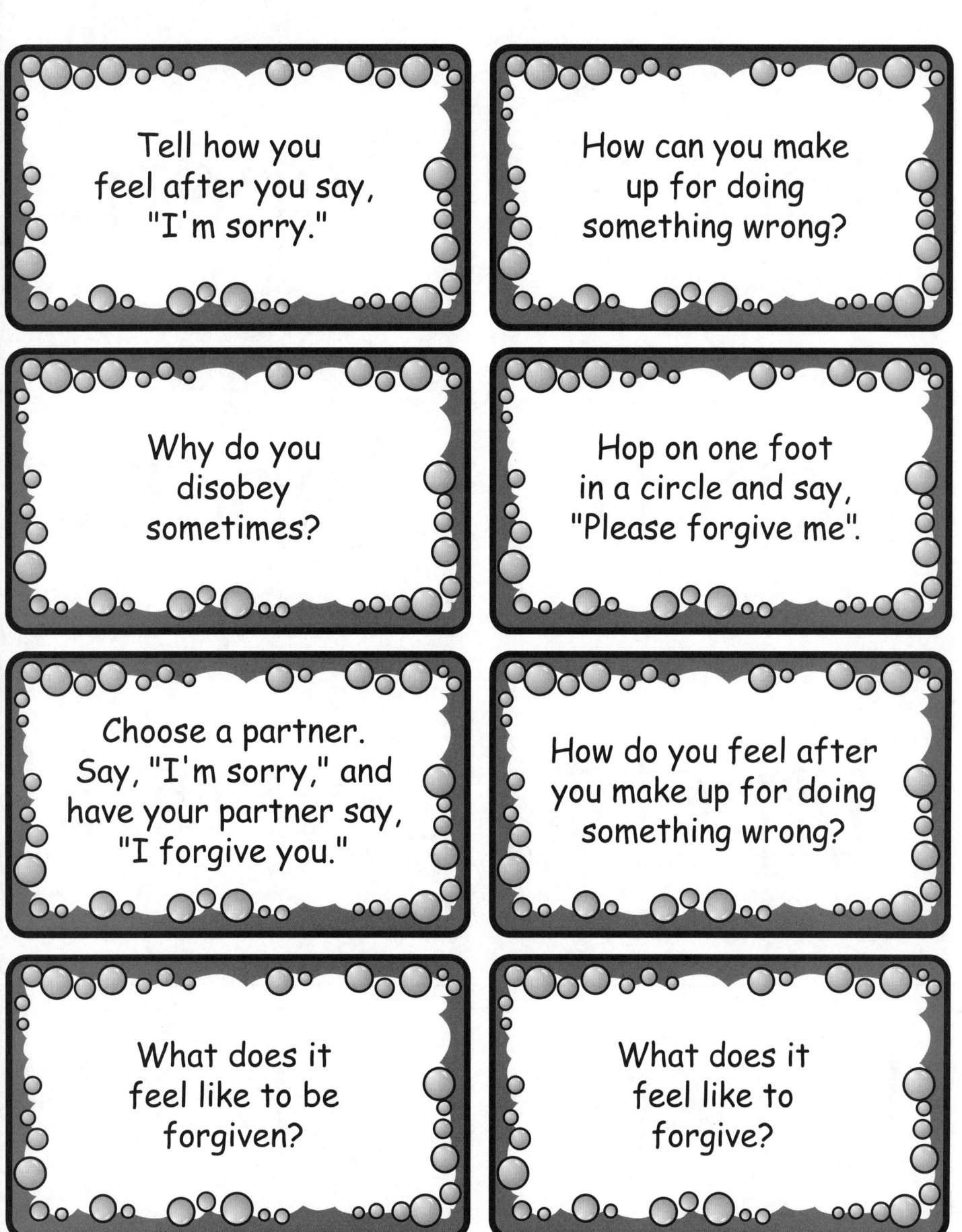

something's fishy 31

TOSS 'N' SHOW

Godprint: Wonder

Players: 2 teams of 3 or more players

The Bible is full of amazing stories about what God has done. The goal of this game is to guess the Bible stories the other team presents. To play you'll need some nickels and some pennies.

Put It Together

1. Cut out the game title (above) and glue it to the front of the folder.
2. Glue "How to Play" (page 35) to the back of the folder.
3. Glue page 38 to the left inside of the folder. Glue page 39 to the right inside of the folder.
4. Add color and laminate as desired.

GET LIST:
- scissors
- glue
- colored markers or pencils

toss 'n show 33

Glue to the front of the game folder

How to Play

GET LIST: ◆ 10 pennies ◆ 10 nickels
◆ scrap paper ◆ pencils (watch or minute timer)

1. Set the open gameboard on the floor. Form two teams. Give one team 10 pennies and the other team 10 nickels.

2. Decide which team will go first. The first player will stand two steps away from the gameboard. Toss a coin. Try to make it land in one of the spaces.

3. Look at the picture on the space you land on. The picture tells you what kind of story you'll tell. You can use as many people from your team as you'd like. You may act out the story without words or you may draw pictures from the story on scrap paper.

- A story about water.
- A story with an angel.
- A story that has food in it.
- A story with a miracle.
- A story about a king or queen.
- A story about Jesus.
- Free choice.

4. Set a timer for one minute or have one person keep time with a watch. (If you think one minute is not enough, you can choose another time limit.) The other team will try to guess which Bible story you are acting out or drawing. If they guess before time is up, you get to leave your coin on that space. If the other team does not guess your story, remove your coin and try again later.

5. Now the other team takes a turn tossing a coin on the gameboard. Try to make it land in a space without a coin. Play until all the spaces have either a penny or a nickel. Count up the coins to see which team wins.

Cut out these rules and glue them to the back of the game folder.

toss 'n show

35

Glue playing rules to back of folder.

Glue inside the left side of the game folder.

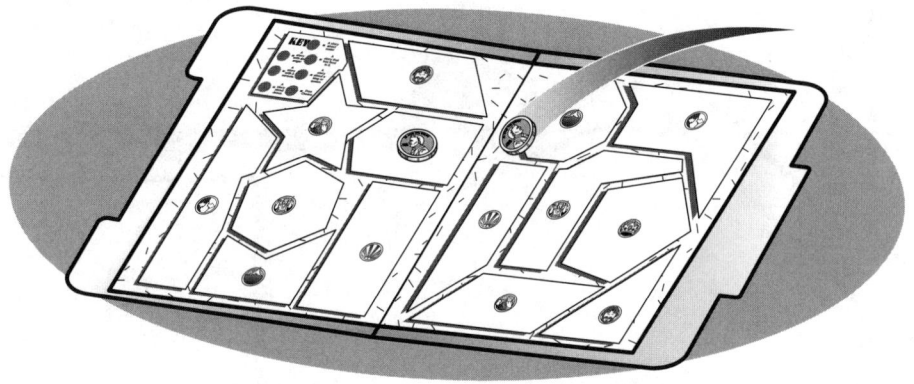

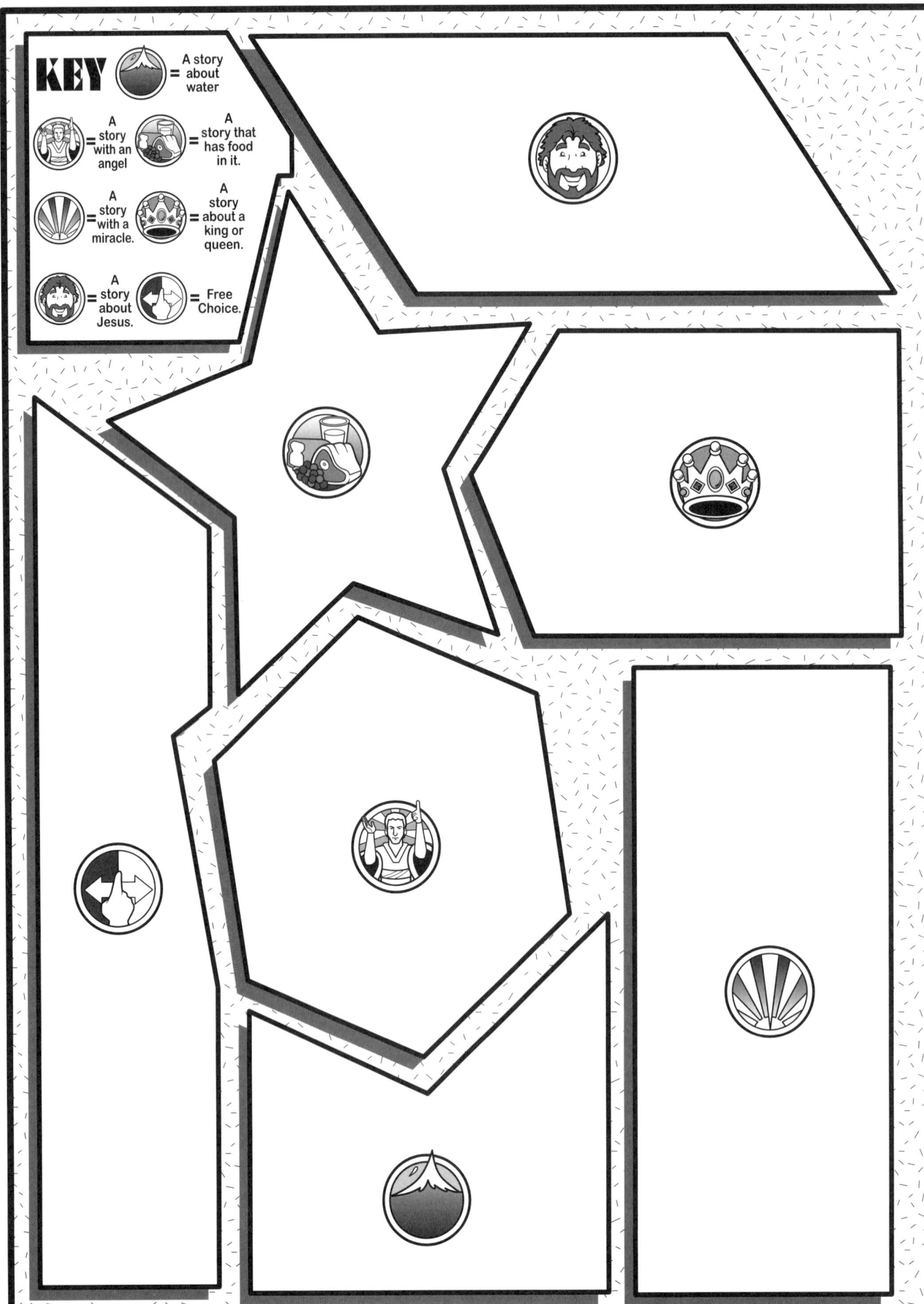

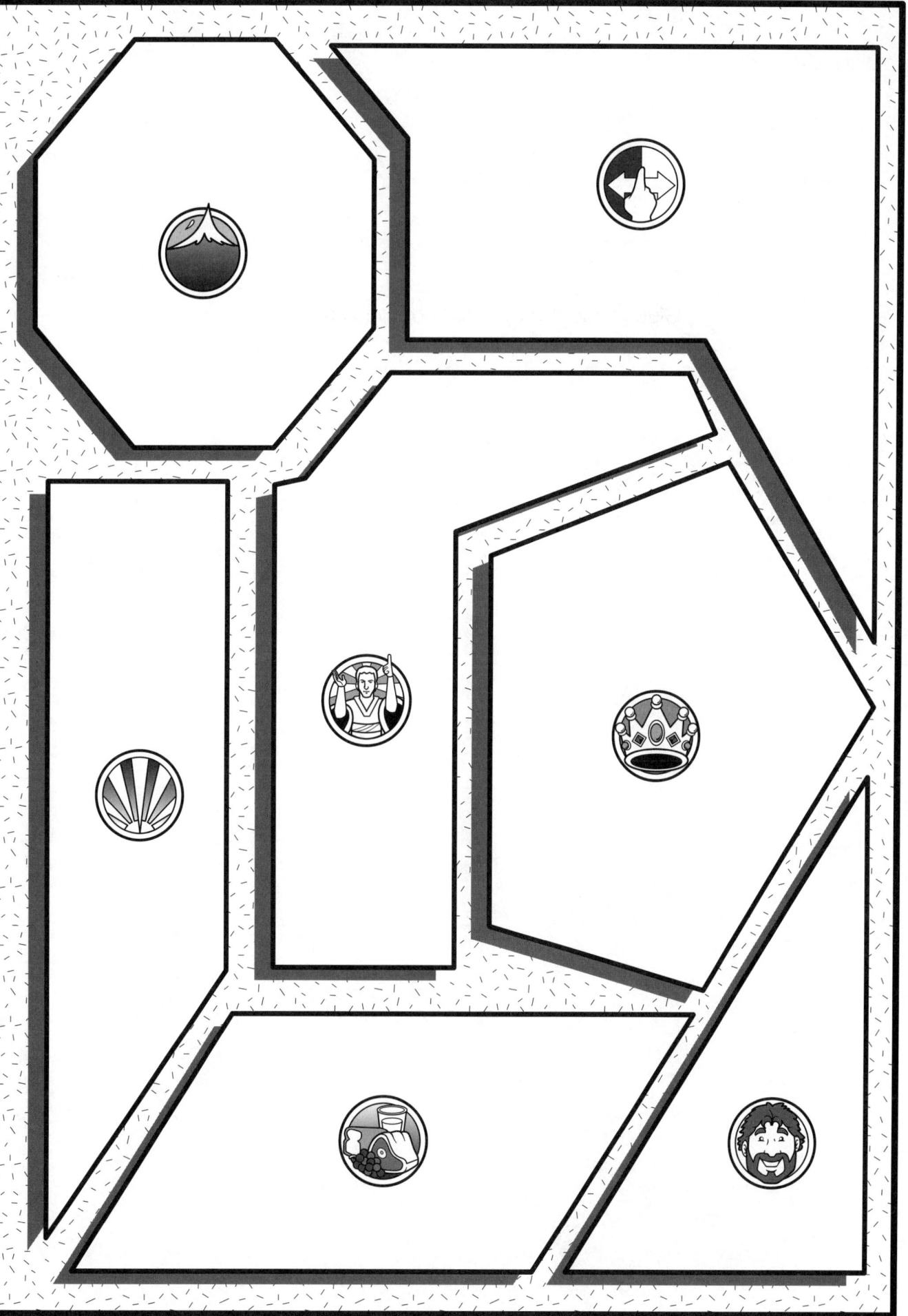

Glue inside the right side of the game folder.

PICTURE THAT!

Godprint: Praise **Players:** 4 players

A picture is worth a thousand words! Use geometric shapes to make pictures that help you remember Bible stories and praise God for his greatness.

Put It Together

1. Cut out the game title (above) and glue it to the front of the folder.
2. Glue "How to Play" (page 43) to the back of the folder. Leave space above the rules to glue a zip-top bag or envelope to the folder. 
3. Glue page 46 inside the left side of the game folder. Glue page 47 to the right side. Add color to the shape pictures. Choose four colors that match the colors of your index cards and use one color for each shape.
4. Cut out the shape patterns on page 49 and use them to cut 12 of each shape from the colored index cards. Use one color for each shape, and match to the colors you added to the gameboard. Store shapes for playing in the zip-top bag on the back of the folder.

GET LIST:
- colorful index cards
- scissors
- glue
- zip-top bag or envelope
- markers or colored pencils

picture that! 41

Glue to the front of the game folder.

How to Play

1. Mix all the shapes together and give each player 12 pieces.

2. Choose one of the story pictures you see inside the folder. Look up the story in the Bible and read it aloud together.

3. Following the pattern in the game folder, use your shapes to make a picture. Decide who will go first. The first player starts by putting down one of the shapes on the center "spine" of the picture. Take turns until the spine is finished.

4. Next start adding to the sides. Here's the tricky part. As a group, you must add to both sides evenly. If a player adds a shape to one side, the next player must add the same shape to the other side so that the two halves look the same. If you don't have the right piece, say "Pass" and let the next player take a turn.

5. If the two halves of the picture look the same, then you can add a shape to a new part of the picture. You must connect to one of the pieces already laid down.

6. Play until the picture is finished.

7. Before you put the game away, talk about the questions in the middle of the gameboard.

If you'd like, use the shapes to make a picture of another favorite Bible story.

Cut out these playing rules and glue them to the back of the game folder.

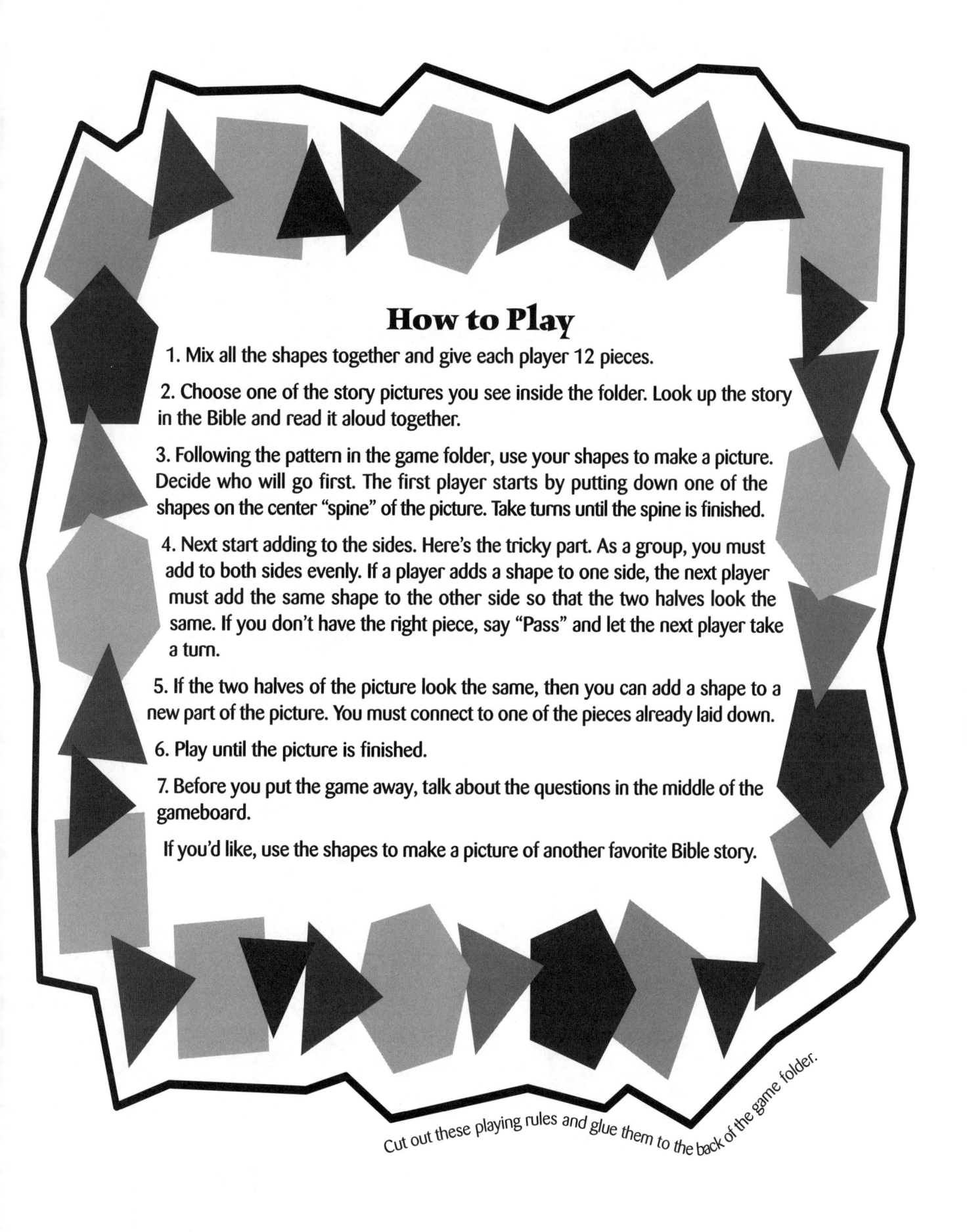

picture that! 43

Glue to the back of the game folder.

Glue to the left inside of the game folder.

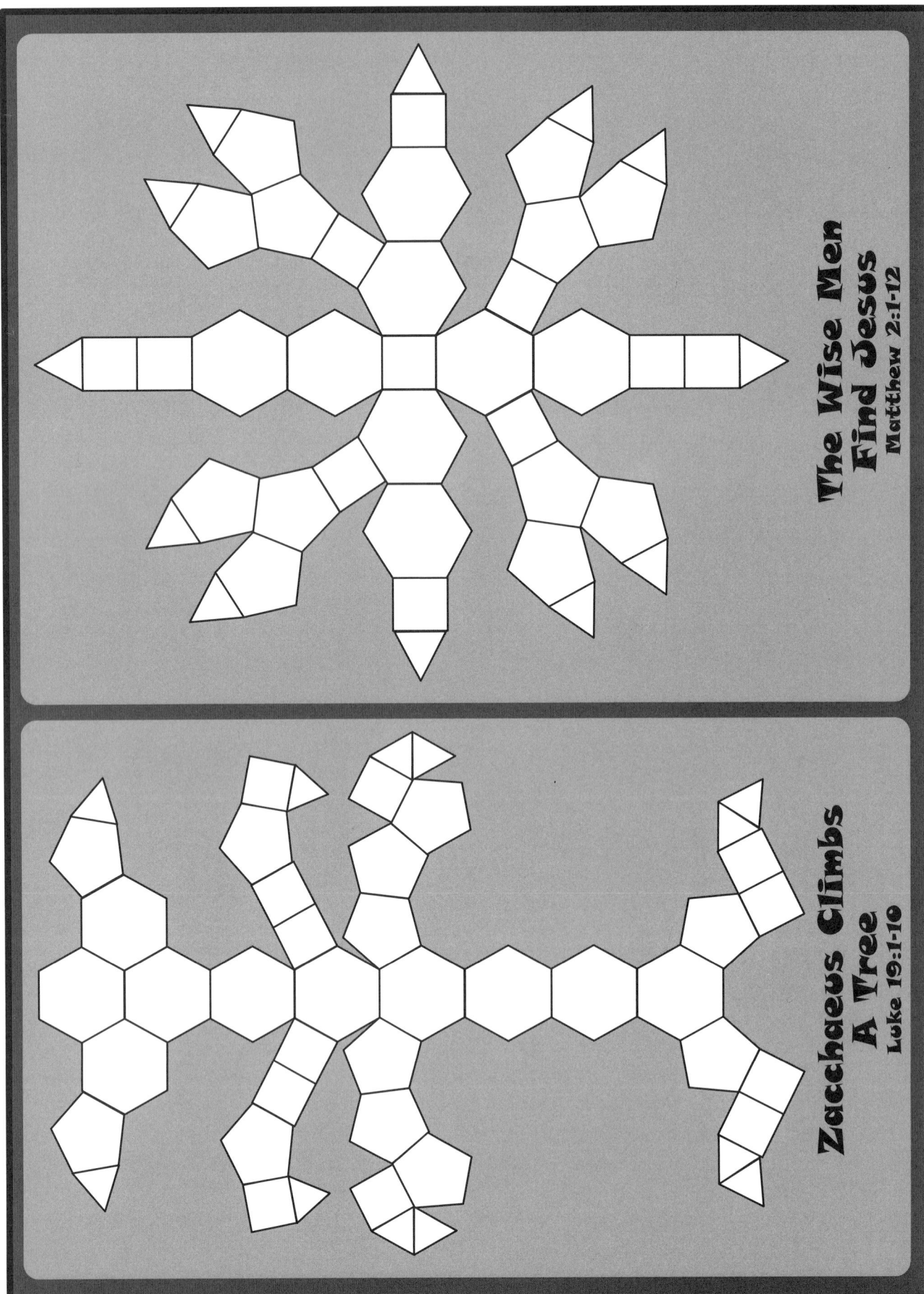

- How does the picture you made remind you of the story?
- What will you remember most about this story?

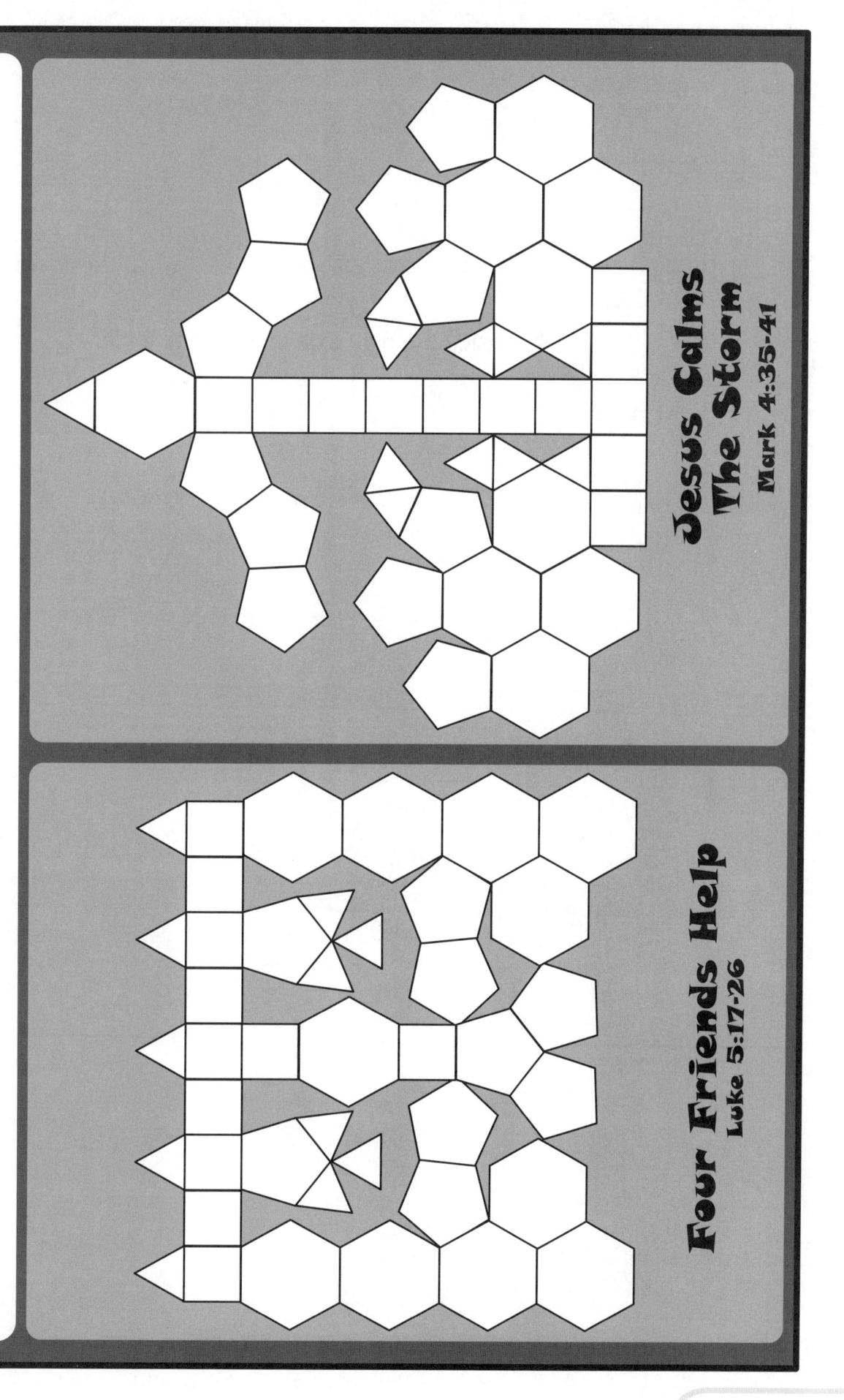

Jesus Calms The Storm
Mark 4:35-41

- Who believed in Jesus in this story?
- How did Jesus help someone in this story?

Four Friends Help
Luke 5:17-26

picture that!

47

Glue inside the right side of the game folder.

Use these patterns and cut 12 of each shape from colorful index cards. Use one color for each shape. Match to the colors you add to the same shapes on the gameboard.

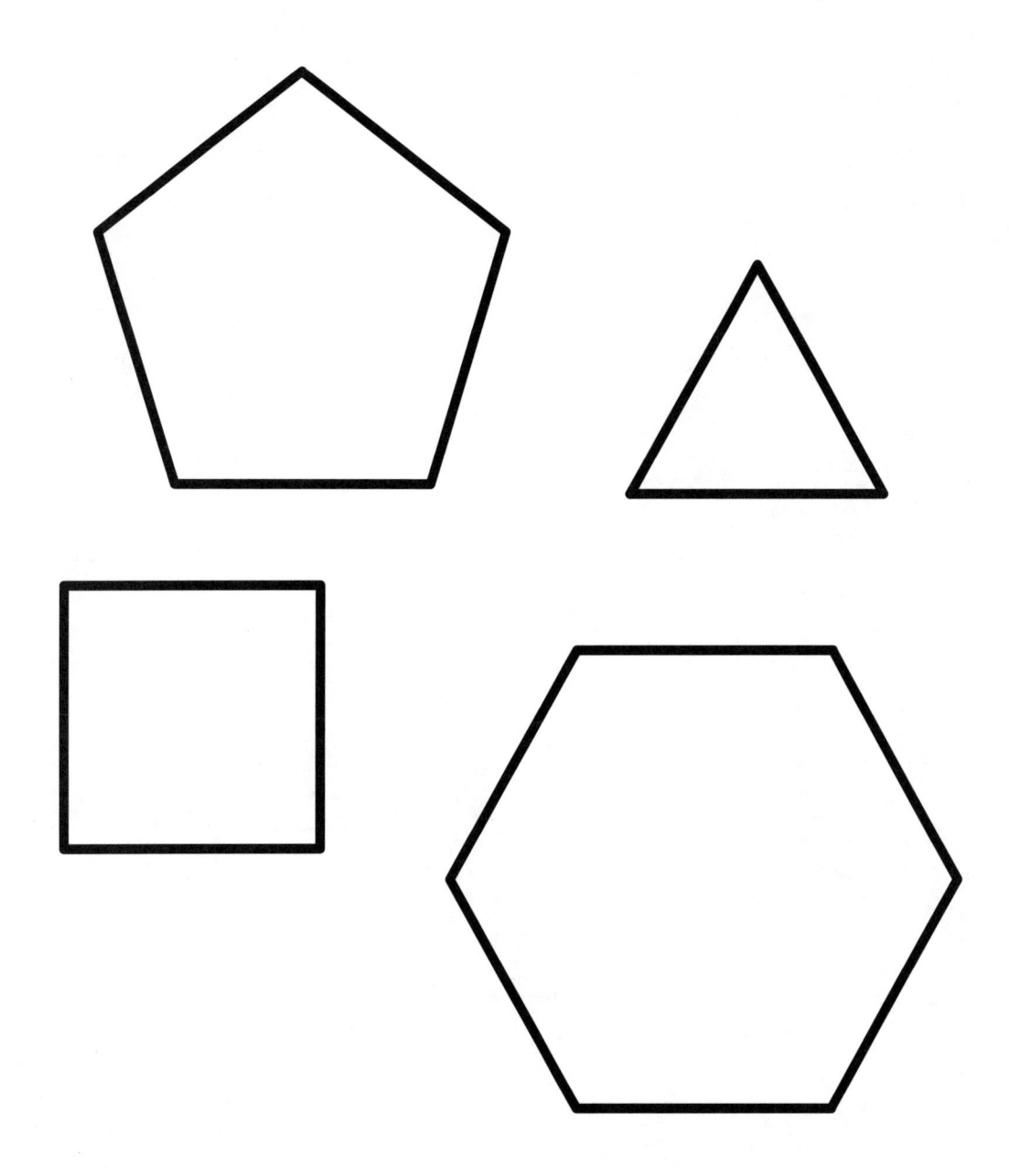

picture that!

UP THE MOUNTAIN

Godprint: Discipleship

Players: 2-6

In the Sermon on the Mount, Jesus talked to a crowd of people about how God wants them to live. This game will help you remember what Jesus said.

Put It Together

1. Cut out the game title (above) and glue it to the front of the folder.

2. Glue "How to Play" (page 53) to the back of the folder.

3. Glue page 56 to the left inside of the folder. Glue page 57 to the right inside of the folder. Add color as desired.

4. Cut out the spinner and arrow from page 59. Use a metal brad to assemble. For a stronger spinner, you may want to glue the spinner to a piece of a file folder cut to the same shape.

GET LIST:
- metal brad
- scissors
- glue
- markers or colored pencils

up the mountain

Glue to the front of the game folder.

How to Play

GET LIST: ♦ beans or buttons for game markers ♦ coin to toss

1. Give each player a bean or button as a game marker.

2. For each turn, toss a coin. If it comes up "heads," move one space. If it comes up "tails," move two spaces. Then read the words on the space you land on and follow the directions.

3. If you land on a stone on the path, spin the spinner and do what it says.

4. Play until everyone reaches the top of the mountain.

Cut out these rules and glue them to the back of the game folder.

Glue playing rules to the back of the game folder.

Glue inside the left side of the game folder.

TRUST GOD LOOP

Read Matthew 7:7. Follow Trust God Loop.

If you don't listen to Jesus, you are foolish. Go back 2.

Read Matthew 6:33 Tell one way to put God's Kingdom first.

You're worried whether your clothes are cool. Read Matthew 6:25 and Slide down Worry Trail.

Jesus explained that God takes care of what we need. Tell one way that God takes care of you.

You promised your teacher you would do your homework, but you didn't. **Go Back 1**

You were angry and called someone a name. Go back 2.

You prayed for someone who was mean to you. Go ahead 1.

GOOD THOUGHTS RIVULET

Your teacher was unfair to you, but you kept a good attitude. **Slide up Good Thoughts Rivulet.**

You had a fight with your sister and said you wished she had never been born. **Slide down Bad Thoughts Creek.**

Your friend said something mean about you. You wanted to get even, but you decided to forgive. **Go ahead 3 spaces.**

BAD THOUGHT

Large crowds followed Jesus. So he sat down on a mountain to teach them.

START

Jesus finished teaching. The crowds were amazed!

If you do what Jesus says, you are wise. Go ahead 1.

Read Matthew 6:9-13 Tell your favorite part of the Lord's Prayer.

Read Matthew 6:6 Tell how God wants us to pray.

WORRY TRAIL

You told someone you were sorry and made friends again. Go ahead 3.

You wanted everyone to know how much money you gave for needy people. Go back 2.

Jesus explained how God wants people to pray.

You had a disagreement with a friend and didn't speak to each other for a week. Go back 2.

Jesus told the people how they should treat others.

CREEK

In the Beatitudes, Jesus talked about being truly happy on the inside. Tell how God makes you happy inside.

Read Matthew 5:13. Tell why salt is important.

Read Matthew 5:14. Explain what you think Jesus means.

Glue inside the right side of the game folder.

Prayer Wheel

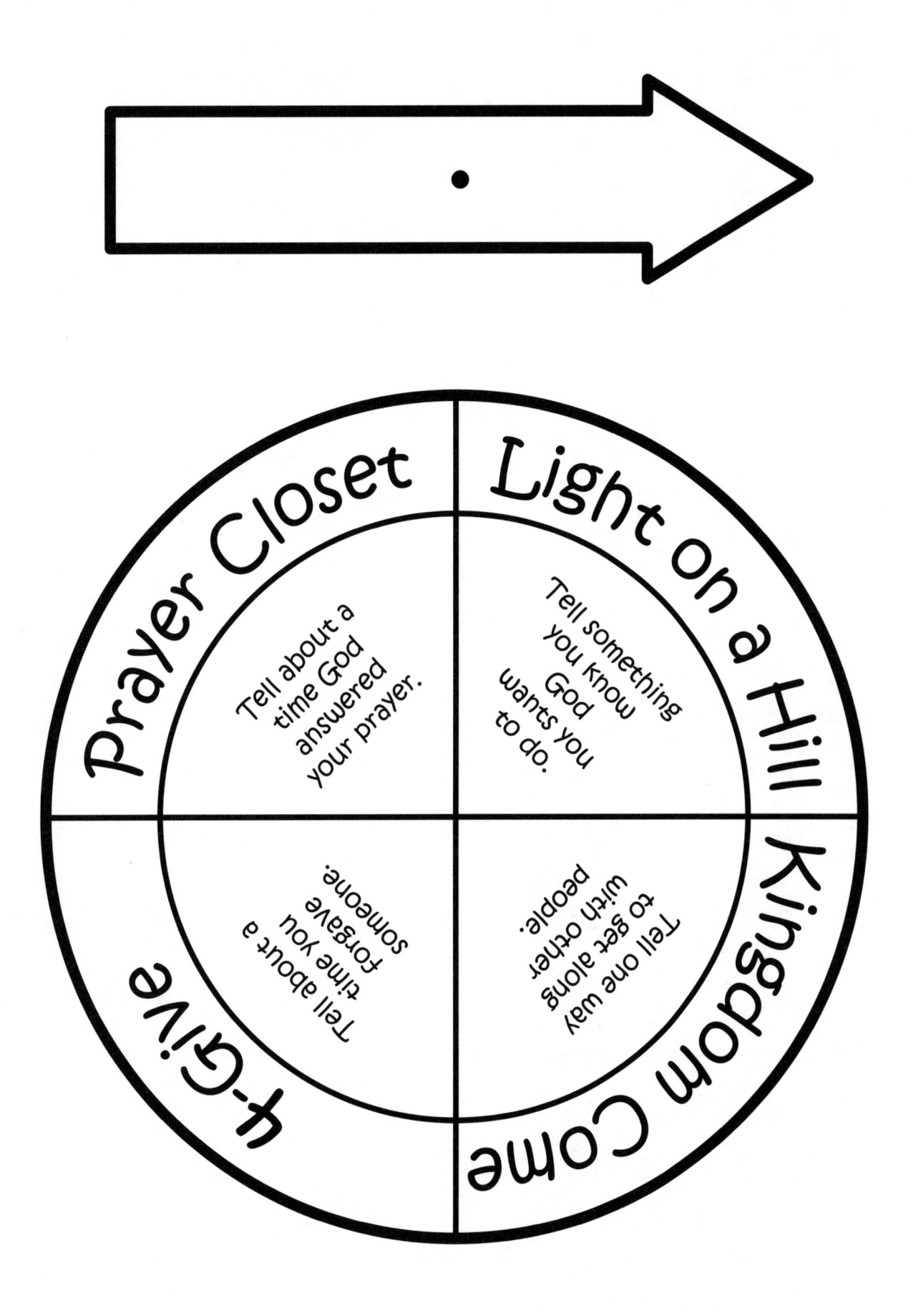

Prayer Closet — Tell about a time God answered your prayer.

Light on a Hill — Tell something you know God wants you to do.

Kingdom Come — Tell one way to get along with other people.

4-Give — Tell about a time you forgave someone.

up the mountain

59

On the Move with Moses

Godprint: Faithfulness

Players: 2 Teams any Size

God faithfully protected Moses, and Moses became a leader of God's people. Find out how much you remember about the faithful life of Moses as he followed God and led the people.

Put It Together

1. Cut out the game title (above) and glue it to the front of the folder.

2. Glue "How to Play" (page 63) to the back of the folder.

3. Glue page 66 to the left inside of the folder. Glue page 67 to the right inside of the folder. Add color as desired.

4. Cut apart the "Stick to the Basics" and "Meet the Challenge" cards on pages 69–78.

GET LIST:
- glue
- scissors
- markers or colored pencils

on the move with moses

Glue to front of game folder.

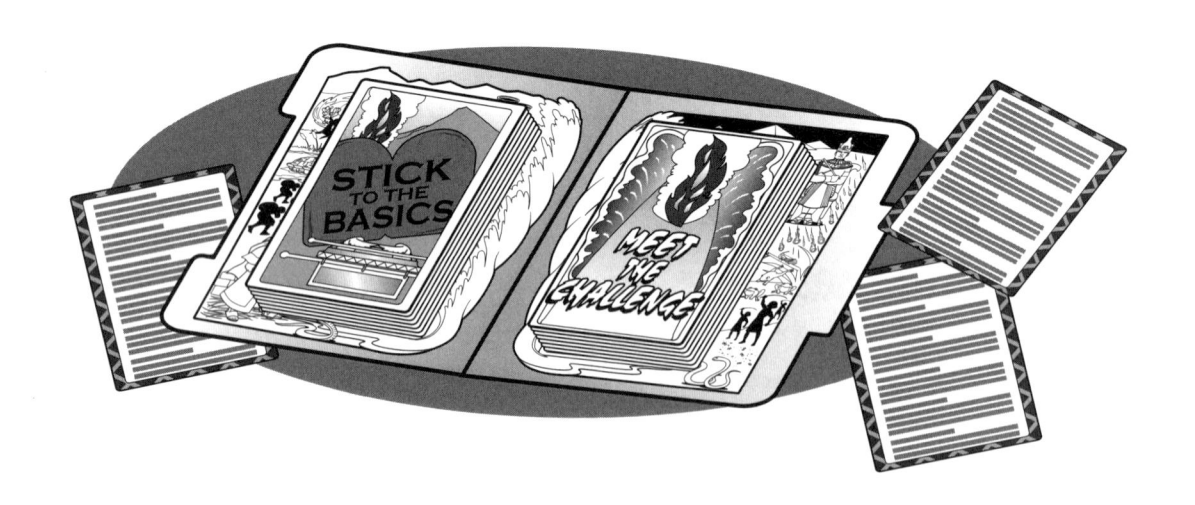

folder games

How to Play

GET LIST:
- paper and pencil to keep score
- watch with second hand or a one-minute timer

1. Choose a person to be "host" of the game. Choose someone else to keep score. Choose a third person to keep time. (If your group is small, the scorekeeper and timekeeper can also play.)

2. Make two even teams. When it's your team's turn, choose one of the game cards. You can choose a "Stick to the Basics" card for 5 points per question or a "Meet the Challenge" card for 10 points per question. The "Meet the Challenge" cards are worth more points because the questions are harder.

3. The timekeeper will say "Go." The host will read the questions from your card. Your team will answer as many questions as you can in one minute. If you do not know the answer, say "Pass" and keep trying to answer questions. After one minute, the timekeeper calls "Stop." The scorekeeper will give points for correct answers. If you answer all 10 questions in one minute, you get 50 bonus points.

4. Play until you use all the question cards. Find out which team has the most points.

5. To play another way, allow more time and have players look up the Bible references for each question.

Cut out these playing rules and glue them to the back of the game folder.

Glue playing rules to back of game folder.

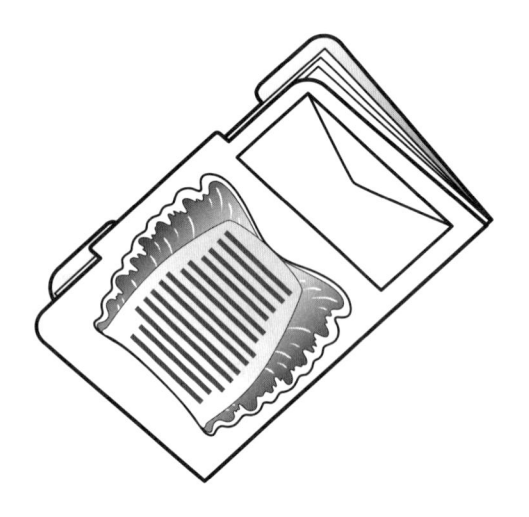

Glue inside left side of the game folder.

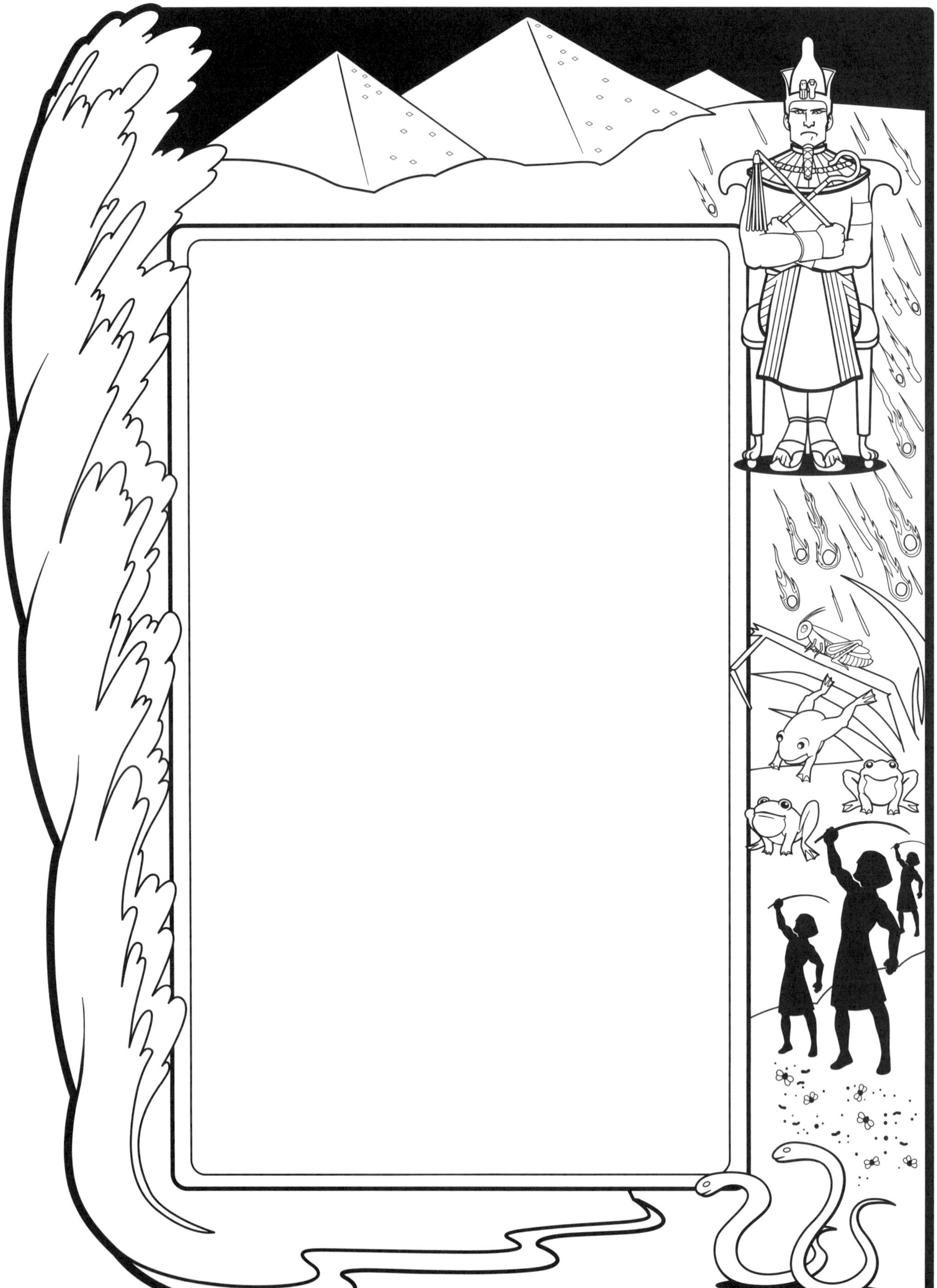

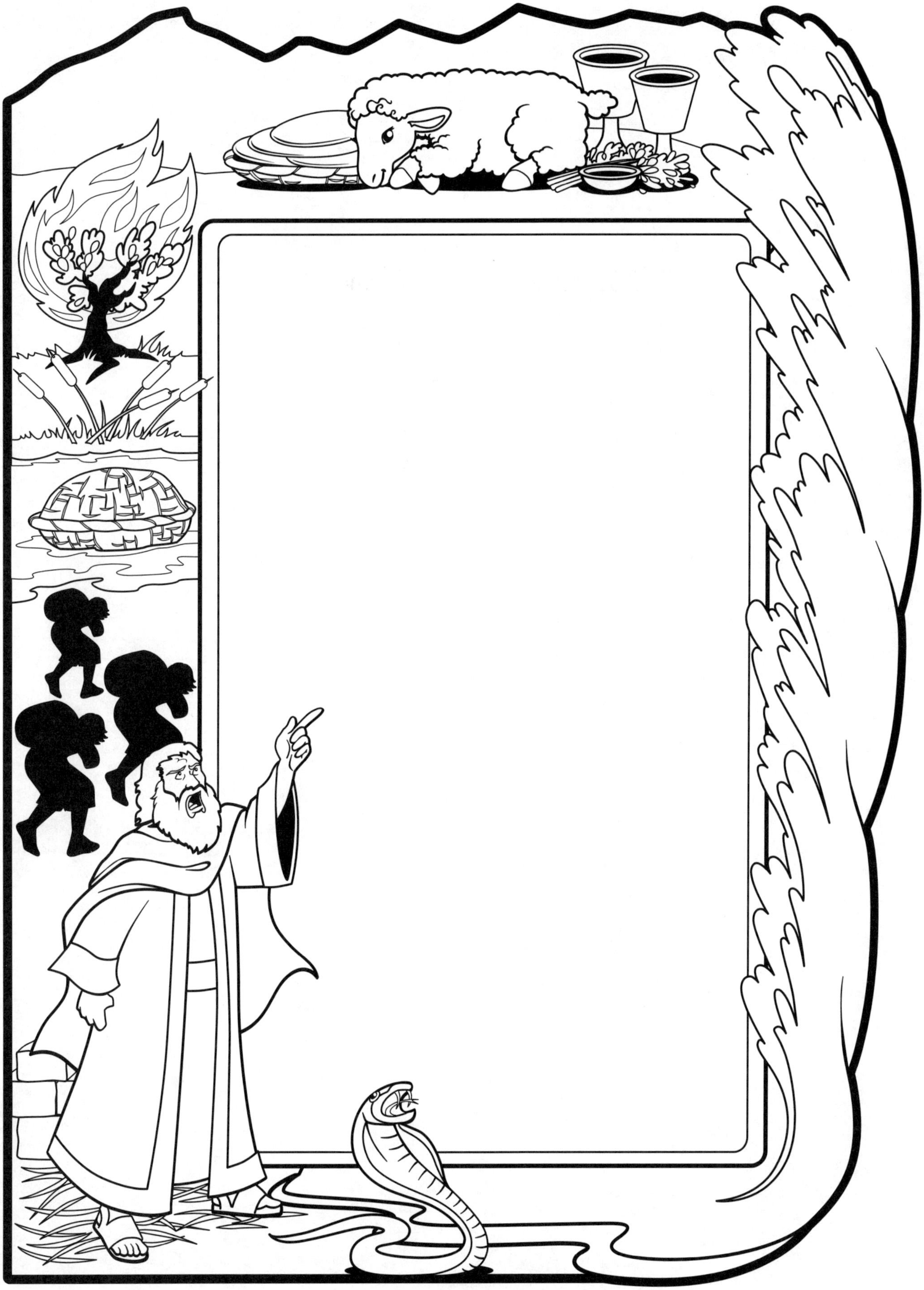

Glue inside right side of game folder.

1. TRUE OR FALSE: THE KING OF EGYPT WANTED ALL THE HEBREW BABIES TO DIE. (FALSE. HE WANTED ONLY THE BOYS TO DIE. Ex. 1:22)

2. HOW DID THE KING OF EGYPT WANT TO KILL HEBREW BABIES? (THROW THEM IN THE NILE. Ex. 1:22)

3. TRUE OR FALSE: MOSES' FAMILY WERE SLAVES. (TRUE. ALL THE HEBREWS WERE SLAVES. Ex. 1:11)

4. HOW LONG DID MOSES' MOTHER HIDE HIM AT HOME? (THREE MONTHS. Ex. 2:2)

5. WHAT WAS THE BASKET MOSES' MOTHER USED MADE OF? (PAPYRUS; STEMS OF TALL GRASS. Ex. 2:3)

6. WHAT WAS THE BASKET MOSES' MOTHER USED COATED WITH? (TAR. Ex. 2:3)

7. WHO WAS WATCHING OVER MOSES IN THE BASKET? (HIS SISTER. Ex. 2:4)

8. WHY DID PHARAOH'S DAUGHTER GO DOWN TO THE RIVER? (TO TAKE A BATH. Ex. 2:5)

9. WHEN PHARAOH'S DAUGHTER OPENED THE BASKET, WHAT WAS MOSES DOING? (CRYING. Ex. 2:6)

10. DID PHARAOH'S DAUGHTER KNOW THIS BABY WAS ONE OF THE HEBREW BABIES? (YES. Ex. 2:6)

---

1. WHAT DID MOSES' SISTER OFFER TO DO FOR PHARAOH'S DAUGHTER? (GET A WOMAN TO TAKE CARE OF THE BABY. Ex. 2:7)

2. TRUE OR FALSE: MOSES' SISTER GOT HIS OWN MOTHER TO TAKE CARE OF HIM. (TRUE. Ex. 2:8)

3. TRUE OR FALSE: PHARAOH'S DAUGHTER PAID MOSES' MOTHER TO TAKE CARE OF THE BABY. (TRUE. Ex. 2:9)

4. TRUE OR FALSE: PHARAOH'S DAUGHTER TOOK MOSES HOME WITH HER WHEN HE WAS A BABY. (FALSE. AS A BABY, MOSES LIVED WITH HIS MOTHER. WHEN HE WAS OLDER, SHE TOOK HIM TO PHARAOH'S DAUGHTER. Ex. 2:10)

5. ONE DAY MOSES SAW AN EGYPTIAN HITTING A HEBREW MAN. WHAT DID HE DO? (HE KILLED THE EGYPTIAN. Ex. 2:12)

6. DID GOD CALL OUT TO MOSES FROM INSIDE THE BUSH? (YES. HE SAID, "MOSES! MOSES!" Ex. 3:4)

7. WHEN MOSES SAW THE BURNING BUSH, WHAT DID GOD TELL HIM TO TAKE OFF? (HIS SANDALS. Ex. 3:5)

8. GOD PROMISED TO TAKE THE HEBREW PEOPLE TO A LAND WITH PLENTY OF MILK AND _____. (HONEY. Ex. 3:8)

9. TRUE OR FALSE: WHEN GOD SPOKE TO MOSES FROM THE BUSH, MOSES WAS GLAD TO DO WHAT GOD ASKED HIM TO DO. (FALSE. MOSES DIDN'T THINK HE WAS THE RIGHT PERSON. Ex. 3:11)

10. WHEN GOD SPOKE TO MOSES FROM THE BUSH, HE SAID HE WAS THE GOD OF ABRAHAM, ISAAC AND _____. (JACOB. Ex. 3:6)

on the move with moses

69

folder games

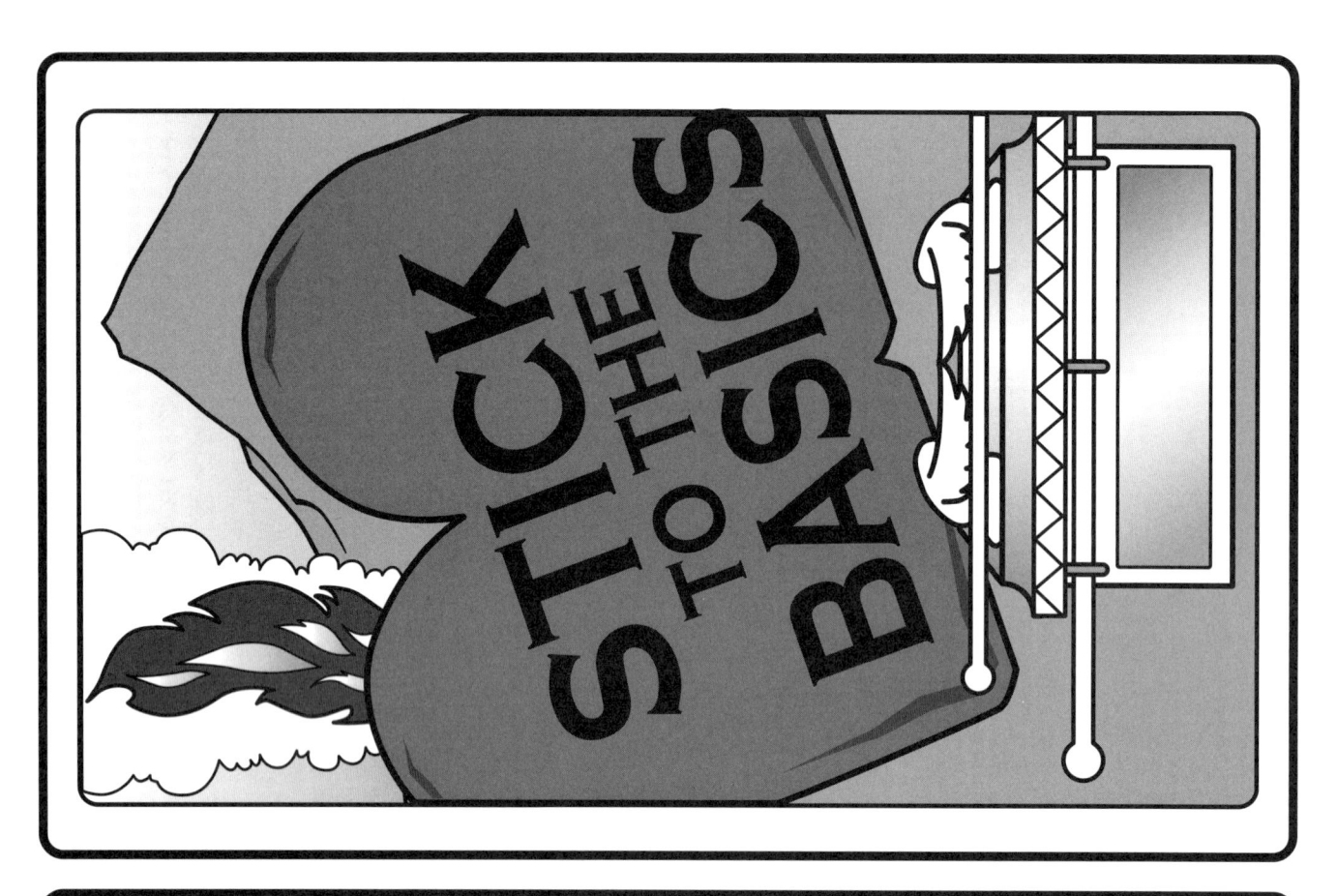

1. TRUE OR FALSE: GOD TOLD MOSES TO THROW HIS STAFF ON THE GROUND. (TRUE. Ex. 4:3)

2. WHAT HAPPENED WHEN MOSES THREW HIS STAFF ON THE GROUND? (IT TURNED INTO A SNAKE. Ex. 4:3).

3. TRUE OR FALSE: GOD TOLD MOSES TO PICK UP THE SNAKE BY ITS HEAD. (FALSE. GOD SAID TO PICK UP THE SNAKE BY ITS TAIL. Ex. 4:4)

4. WHO DID GOD SAY WOULD BE LIKE MOSES' MOUTH? (HIS BROTHER AARON. Ex. 4:16)

5. MOSES TOLD THE ELDERS EVERYTHING GOD HAD TOLD HIM. DID THEY BELIEVE HIM? (YES. Ex. 4:31)

6. AFTER MOSES AND AARON WENT TO SEE PHARAOH, WHAT DID PHARAOH TAKE AWAY FROM THE HEBREW WORKERS? (STRAW TO MAKE BRICKS. Ex. 5:7)

7. AFTER THE HEBREWS HAD TO FIND THEIR OWN STRAW TO MAKE BRICKS WITH, DID THEY HAVE TO MAKE THE SAME NUMBER OF BRICKS AS BEFORE? (YES. Ex. 5:11)

8. THE PEOPLE WERE UPSET THAT MOSES HAD MADE THINGS WORSE FOR THEM. WHAT DID MOSES SAY TO GOD? ("WHY HAVE YOU BROUGHT TROUBLE UPON THIS PEOPLE?...YOU HAVE NOT RESCUED YOUR PEOPLE AT ALL." Ex. 5:22-23)

9. THE LAND THAT GOD PROMISED THE HEBREW PEOPLE WAS CALLED _____. (CANAAN. Ex. 6:4)

10. WHEN GOD TOLD MOSES TO GO TO PHARAOH A SECOND TIME, WHAT DID MOSES SAY? (HE WON'T LISTEN TO ME. I DON'T SPEAK VERY WELL. Ex. 6:12)

---

1. TRUE OR FALSE: GOD PROMISED TO DO MIRACLES IN EGYPT. (TRUE. Ex. 7:3)

2. GOD TOLD AARON TO THROW HIS STAFF DOWN IN FRONT OF PHARAOH. IT TURNED INTO WHAT? (A SNAKE. Ex. 7:10)

3. AFTER TURNING THE RIVER INTO BLOOD, WHAT WAS THE NEXT PLAGUE ON EGYPT? (FROGS. Ex. 8:2)

4. BEFORE HE SENT HAIL, GOD WARNED EVERYONE TO TAKE THEIR ANIMALS INSIDE. DID ANY OF THE EGYPTIANS PAY ATTENTION TO THE WARNING? (YES. Ex. 9:20)

5. DID HAIL FALL ON THE PART OF EGYPT WHERE THE HEBREWS WERE? (NO. Ex. 9:26)

6. HOW LONG DID THE PLAGUE OF DARKNESS LAST? (3 DAYS. Ex. 10:22)

7. WHAT WAS THE TENTH AND FINAL PLAGUE ON EGYPT? (DEATH OF THE FIRSTBORN SON. Ex. 11:5)

8. HOW WERE THE HEBREWS PROTECTED FROM THE LAST PLAGUE? (GOD TOLD THEM TO PUT BLOOD ON THEIR DOORFRAMES. Ex. 12:7)

9. HOW LONG DID THE HEBREW PEOPLE LIVE IN EGYPT? (430 YEARS. Ex. 12:40)

10. WHAT IS THE NAME OF THE CELEBRATION OF THE HEBREWS LEAVING EGYPT? (THE PASSOVER. Ex. 12:43)

on the move with moses

folder games

1. As the Hebrews marched through the desert, what guided them by day? (A pillar of cloud. Ex. 13:21)

2. As the Hebrews marched through the desert, what guided them by night? (A pillar of fire. Ex. 13:21)

3. When the Israelites saw that Pharaoh was chasing them, how did they respond? (They were terrified and complained. Ex. 14:10-11)

4. What did God tell Moses to do to part the waters of the Red Sea so the people could cross? (Hold out his staff. Ex. 14:16)

5. The Egyptians chased the Israelites. What happened when the Egyptians got to the Red Sea? (The waters covered them. Ex. 14:28)

6. Were the people happy with the leadership of Moses and Aaron in the wilderness? (No. They complained. Ex. 16:2)

7. God gave the Israelites manna every morning. How much were they supposed to collect? (Just enough for one day. Ex. 16:4)

8. What kind of meat did God give the people at night? (Quail. Ex. 16:13)

9. What happened when some people tried to collect extra food? (It became rotten. Ex. 16:20)

10. For how many years did the people eat manna? (40. Ex. 16:35)

---

1. When God gave Moses the Ten Commandments, where were the people? (Camped in the desert in front of the mountain. Ex. 19:2)

2. What covered Mount Sinai when God came down on it? (Smoke. Ex. 19:18)

3. True or false: When the people went to meet with God, there was thunder and lightning. (True. Ex. 19:16)

4. True or false: When the people went to meet with God, there was a trumpet blast. (True. Ex. 19:16)

5. What would happen if any of the people tried to go up the mountain to see God? (They would die. Ex. 19:21)

6. Moses took a long time up on the mountain with God. What did the people ask Aaron to do? (Make a golden calf. Ex. 32:1-3)

7. When Moses saw the golden calf, what did he throw down? (The tablets that God had written on. Ex. 32:19)

8. True or false: God gave Moses a new set of stone tablets to replace the ones Moses threw down. (True. Ex. 34:28)

9. What did the people notice about Moses' face when he came down from the mountain? (His face was shining. Ex. 34:29)

10. What did Moses wear to hide his shining face? (A veil. Ex. 34:33)

on the move with moses

73

74 folder games

1. WHAT TRIBE WAS MOSES' FAMILY FROM? (LEVI. Ex. 2:1)

2. TRUE OR FALSE: PHARAOH'S DAUGHTER CAME TO THE RIVER ALONE. (FALSE. HER ATTENDANTS WERE WITH HER. Ex. 2:5)

3. WHO WENT TO GET THE BASKET FROM THE WATER, PHARAOH'S DAUGHTER OR HER SLAVE? (HER SLAVE. Ex. 2:5)

4. DID ANYONE SEE MOSES KILL THE EGYPTIAN MAN? (YES. Ex. 2:14)

5. TRUE OR FALSE: WHEN PHARAOH HEARD THAT MOSES HAD KILLED AN EGYPTIAN MAN, HE TRIED TO KILL MOSES. (TRUE. Ex. 2:15)

6. WHAT WAS THE NAME OF MOSES' WIFE? (ZIPPORAH. Ex. 2:21)

7. TRUE OR FALSE: THE KING WHO WANTED TO KILL MOSES DIED. (TRUE. Ex. 2:23)

8. MOSES RAN AWAY AFTER HE KILLED THE EGYPTIAN MAN. WHAT WAS HIS JOB THEN? (HE WAS A SHEPHERD. Ex. 3:1)

9. TRUE OR FALSE: THERE WAS AN ANGEL IN THE BURNING BUSH THAT MOSES SAW. (TRUE. Ex. 3:2)

10. WHEN GOD CALLED OUT TO MOSES FROM INSIDE THE BUSH, WHAT DID MOSES ANSWER? ("HERE I AM." Ex. 3:4)

---

1. WHEN HE SAW THE BURNING BUSH, WHY DID MOSES HAVE TO TAKE OFF HIS SANDALS? (HE WAS STANDING ON HOLY GROUND. Ex. 3:5)

2. TRUE OR FALSE: GOD TOLD MOSES TO TALK TO HIS OWN FAMILY FIRST. (FALSE. GOD SAID TO GO TO THE ELDERS OF ISRAEL. Ex. 3:16)

3. WHAT WERE THE HEBREW WOMEN SUPPOSED TO ASK FOR BEFORE THEY LEFT EGYPT? (GOLD AND SILVER AND CLOTHES. Ex. 3:22)

4. WHAT WAS MOSES HOLDING IN HIS HAND WHILE HE TALKED TO THE BURNING BUSH? (A WOODEN STAFF. Ex. 4:2)

5. WHAT WAS THE SECOND SIGN THAT GOD GAVE MOSES AT THE BURNING BUSH? (GOD GAVE MOSES' HAND A SKIN DISEASE, THEN HEALED IT. Ex. 4:6-7)

6. WHAT WAS THE NAME OF MOSES' FATHER-IN-LAW? (JETHRO. Ex. 3:1)

7. TRUE OR FALSE: GOD TOLD MOSES THAT EVERYONE WHO WANTED TO KILL HIM WAS DEAD. (TRUE. Ex. 4:19)

8. DID MOSES TAKE ANY CHILDREN WITH HIM WHEN HE WENT BACK TO EGYPT? (YES. HE TOOK HIS SONS. Ex. 4:20)

9. TRUE OR FALSE: GOD SAID HE WOULD MAKE PHARAOH'S HEART STUBBORN. (TRUE. Ex. 4:21)

10. AFTER THE ELDERS OF ISRAEL HEARD WHAT MOSES HAD TO SAY, WHAT DID THEY DO? (BOWED DOWN AND WORSHIPED. Ex. 4:31)

on the move with moses

76 folder games

1. WHEN MOSES AND AARON WENT TO PHARAOH, THEY ASKED PERMISSION TO DO WHAT? (HOLD A FEAST IN GOD'S HONOR IN THE DESERT. Ex. 5:1)

2. HOW OLD WAS MOSES WHEN HE SPOKE TO PHARAOH? (80. Ex. 7:7)

3. TRUE OR FALSE: THE EGYPTIAN MAGICIANS TURNED THEIR STAFFS INTO SNAKES JUST AS AARON HAD. (TRUE. Ex. 7:11)

4. WHAT DID AARON'S STAFF DO TO THE STAFFS OF THE EGYPTIAN MAGICIANS THAT HAD BECOME SNAKES? (SWALLOWED THEM UP. Ex. 7:12)

5. TRUE OR FALSE: ONLY THE NILE RIVER TURNED INTO BLOOD, THE STREAMS AND PONDS STAYED CLEAN. (FALSE: ALL THE WATER TURNED INTO BLOOD. Ex. 7:20)

6. WHO STRUCK THE NILE RIVER WITH HIS STAFF, MOSES OR AARON? (AARON. Ex. 7:20)

7. AFTER THE NILE RIVER TURNED TO BLOOD, WHERE DID THE EGYPTIANS GET DRINKING WATER? (THEY DUG HOLES IN THE GROUND. Ex. 7:24)

8. WHAT WAS THE FIRST PLAGUE THAT THE EGYPTIAN MAGICIANS COULD NOT IMITATE? (THE PLAGUE OF GNATS. Ex. 8:18)

9. BLOOD, FROGS, GNATS, FLIES, LIVESTOCK. WHAT WAS THE NEXT PLAGUE? (BOILS. Ex. 9:9)

10. WHAT STARTED THE PLAGUE OF BOILS? (MOSES AND AARON THREW ASHES FROM A FURNACE. Ex. 9:10)

---

1. THE LOCUST CAME AND ATE UP EVERYTHING. THEN WHAT HAPPENED TO THEM? (A WIND BLEW THEM INTO THE SEA. Ex. 10:19)

2. TRUE OR FALSE: PHARAOH'S OFFICIALS RECOMMENDED THAT HE LET THE PEOPLE GO. (TRUE. Ex. 10:7)

3. WAS IT DAY OR NIGHT WHEN PHARAOH DECIDED TO LET THE PEOPLE GO? (NIGHT. Ex. 12:31)

4. WHAT DID THE MANNA THAT GOD GAVE THE PEOPLE TASTE LIKE? (WAFERS MADE WITH HONEY. Ex. 16:31)

5. TRUE OR FALSE: THE PEOPLE WASHED THEIR CLOTHES TO GET READY TO MEET GOD. (TRUE. Ex. 19:14)

6. WHEN THE PEOPLE MADE A GOLDEN CALF, WHAT DID GOD SAY HE WOULD DO? (DESTROY THEM. Ex. 32:10)

7. WHY DIDN'T GOD DESTROY THE PEOPLE FOR MAKING A GOLDEN CALF? (MOSES ASKED GOD TO HAVE PITY ON THE PEOPLE. Ex. 32:11-12)

8. HOW DID GOD PUNISH THE PEOPLE FOR MAKING THE GOLDEN CALF? (GOD STRUCK THEM WITH A PLAGUE. Ex. 32:35)

9. DID MOSES EVER SEE THE FACE OF GOD? (NO. HE SAW THE BACK OF GOD. Ex. 33:23)

10. WHO DIED FIRST, MOSES OR AARON? (AARON. DEUT. 32:50)

on the move with moses

MEET THE CHALLENGE

MEET THE CHALLENGE

WANDERIN' THE WILDERNESS

Godprint: Faithfulness

Players: 2 or more players or teams

Leaving Egypt—the land of slavery—and entering the land God promised his people was no easy task! It took faithfulness to follow God's leading. Learn the Bible story as you and your friends are "Wanderin' the Wilderness!"

Put It Together

1. Tape together two colorful folders to create one long gameboard. You may want to trim off the top tabs of the folders. This will give you two flat edges to tape together. Use packing tape for added durability.

2. Glue the game title (above) on to the front cover of the folded gameboard. Glue "How to Play" from page 81 to the back cover of the folded gameboard. Leave room to glue an envelope or zip-top bag above the rules in which to store the game cards.

3. Carefully remove the four gameboard panels (pages 84, 85, 88 and 89). Glue them to the inside of the long colorful folder to create the Wanderin' the Wilderness gameboard.

4. Remove the two pages of pop-ups (pages 91 and 93). Cut out each pop-up and assemble as indicated. Tape or glue each pop-up to the gameboard as indicated. Each pop-up will lie flat when the gameboard is folded closed.

5. Remove the three pages of Wilderness Cards (pages 95, 97 and 99). Store the cards in the envelope or zip-top bag on the back covers.

GET LIST:
- 2 colorful folders
- glue stick
- scissors
- packing tape or clear tape
- envelope or zip-top bag

wanderin' the wilderness

Glue to the front of the game folder.

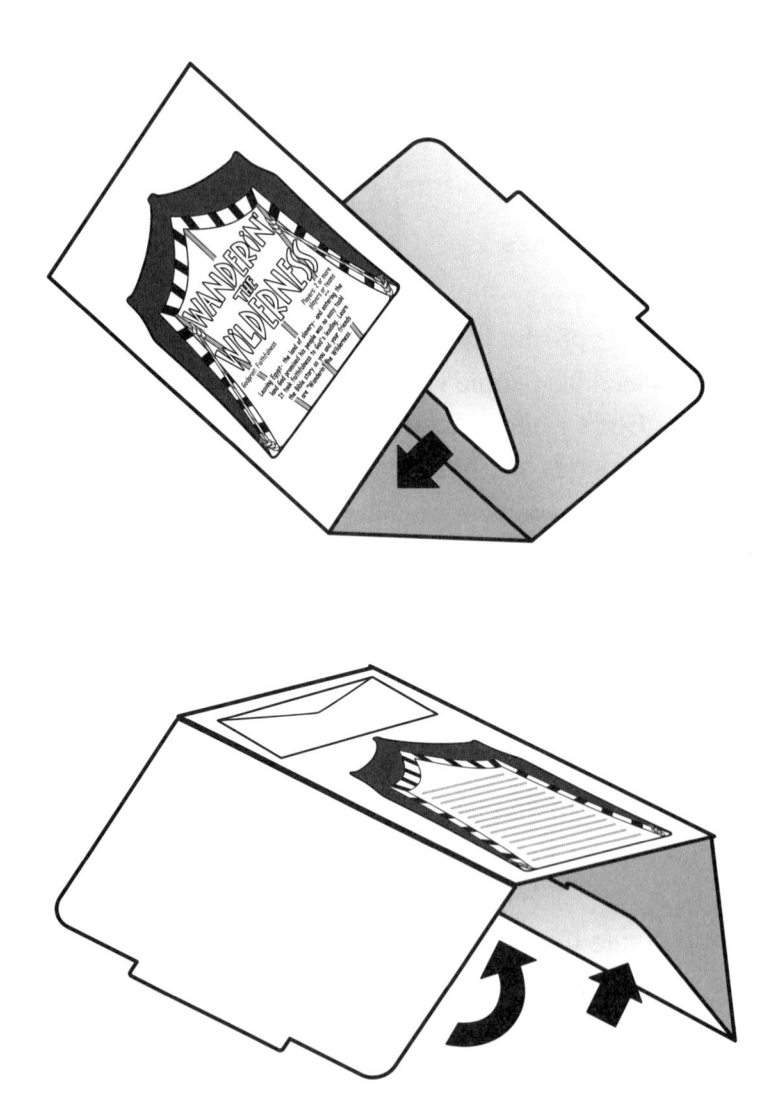

folder games

How to Play

GET LIST:

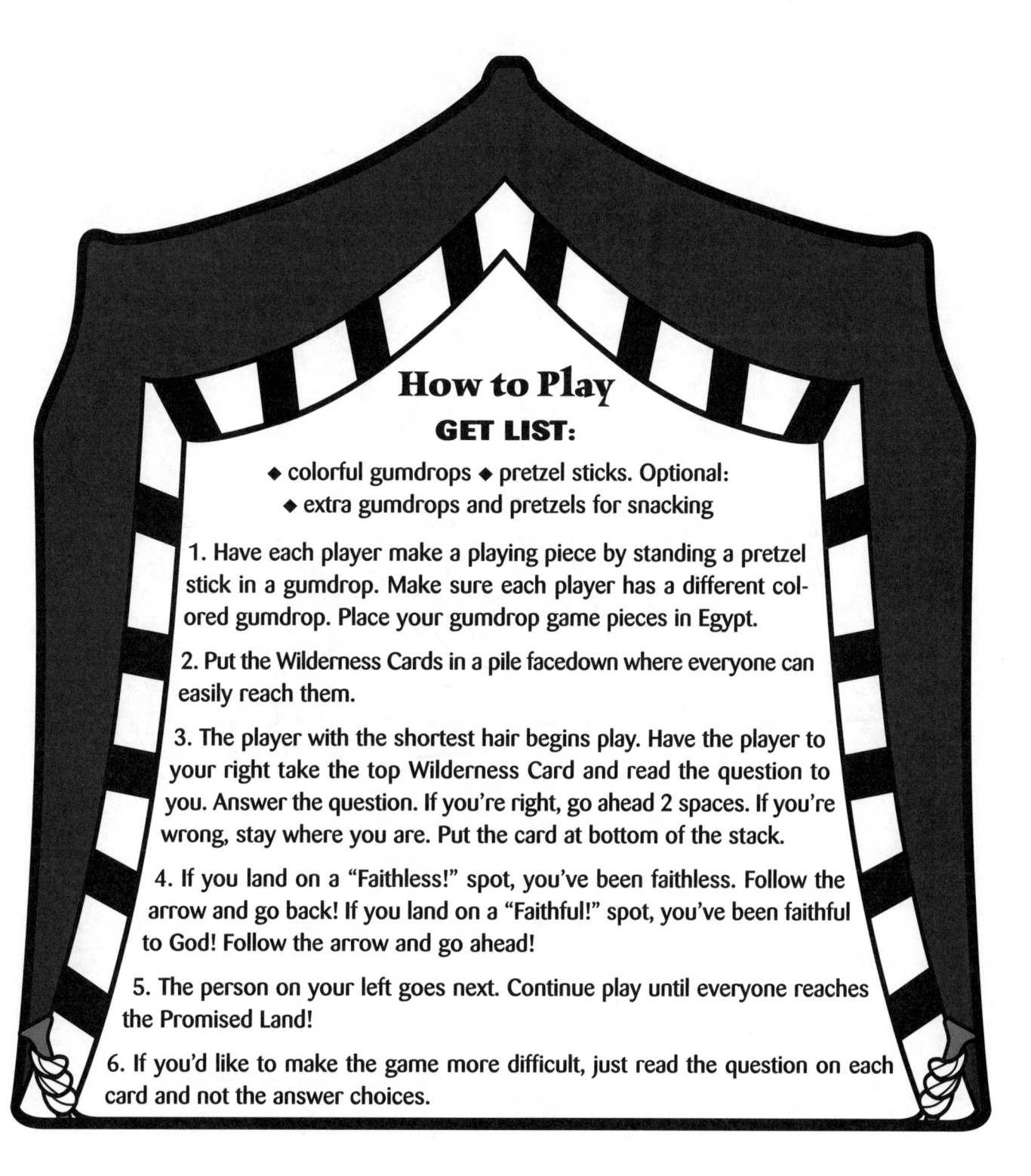

◆ colorful gumdrops ◆ pretzel sticks. Optional:
◆ extra gumdrops and pretzels for snacking

1. Have each player make a playing piece by standing a pretzel stick in a gumdrop. Make sure each player has a different colored gumdrop. Place your gumdrop game pieces in Egypt.

2. Put the Wilderness Cards in a pile facedown where everyone can easily reach them.

3. The player with the shortest hair begins play. Have the player to your right take the top Wilderness Card and read the question to you. Answer the question. If you're right, go ahead 2 spaces. If you're wrong, stay where you are. Put the card at bottom of the stack.

4. If you land on a "Faithless!" spot, you've been faithless. Follow the arrow and go back! If you land on a "Faithful!" spot, you've been faithful to God! Follow the arrow and go ahead!

5. The person on your left goes next. Continue play until everyone reaches the Promised Land!

6. If you'd like to make the game more difficult, just read the question on each card and not the answer choices.

Glue to back of the game folder.

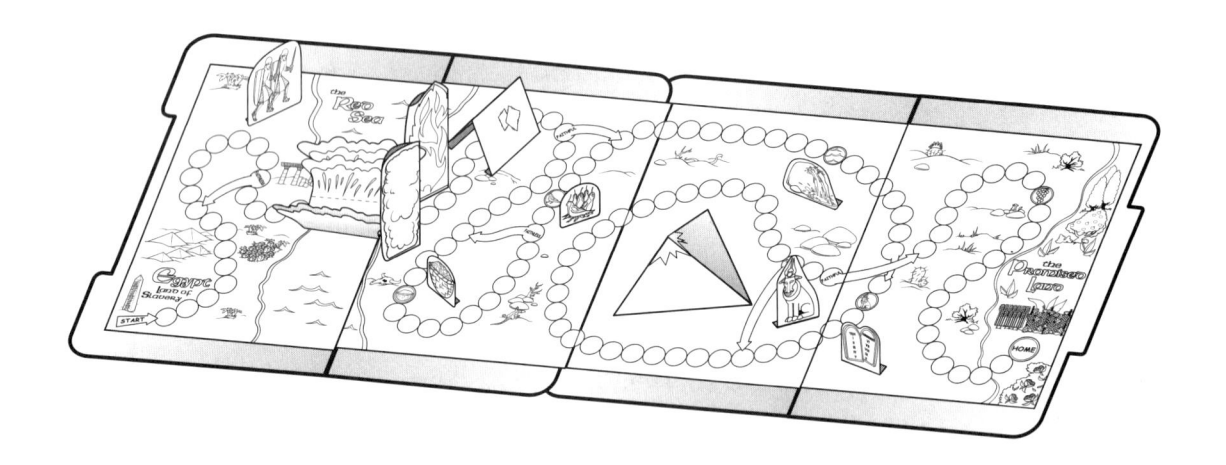

Panel 1. Glue to the far left panel of the gameboard.

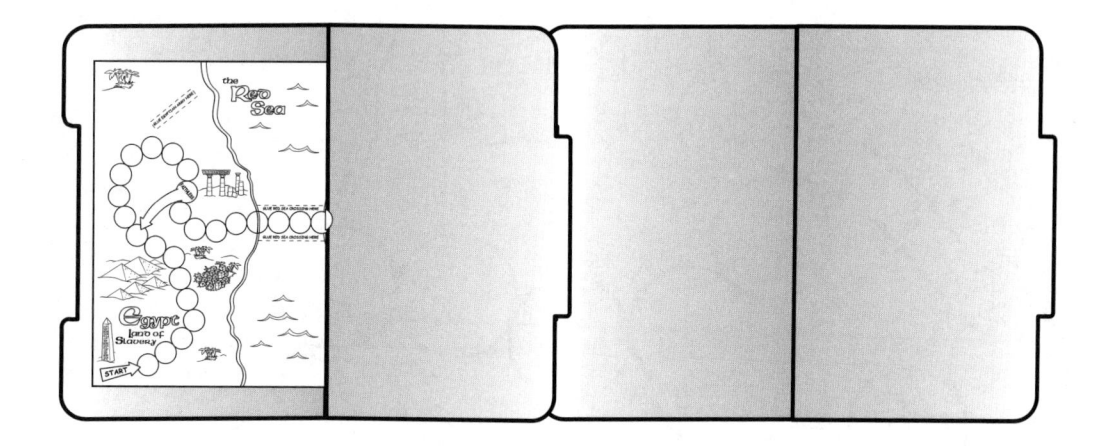

wanderin' the wilderness

the Red Sea

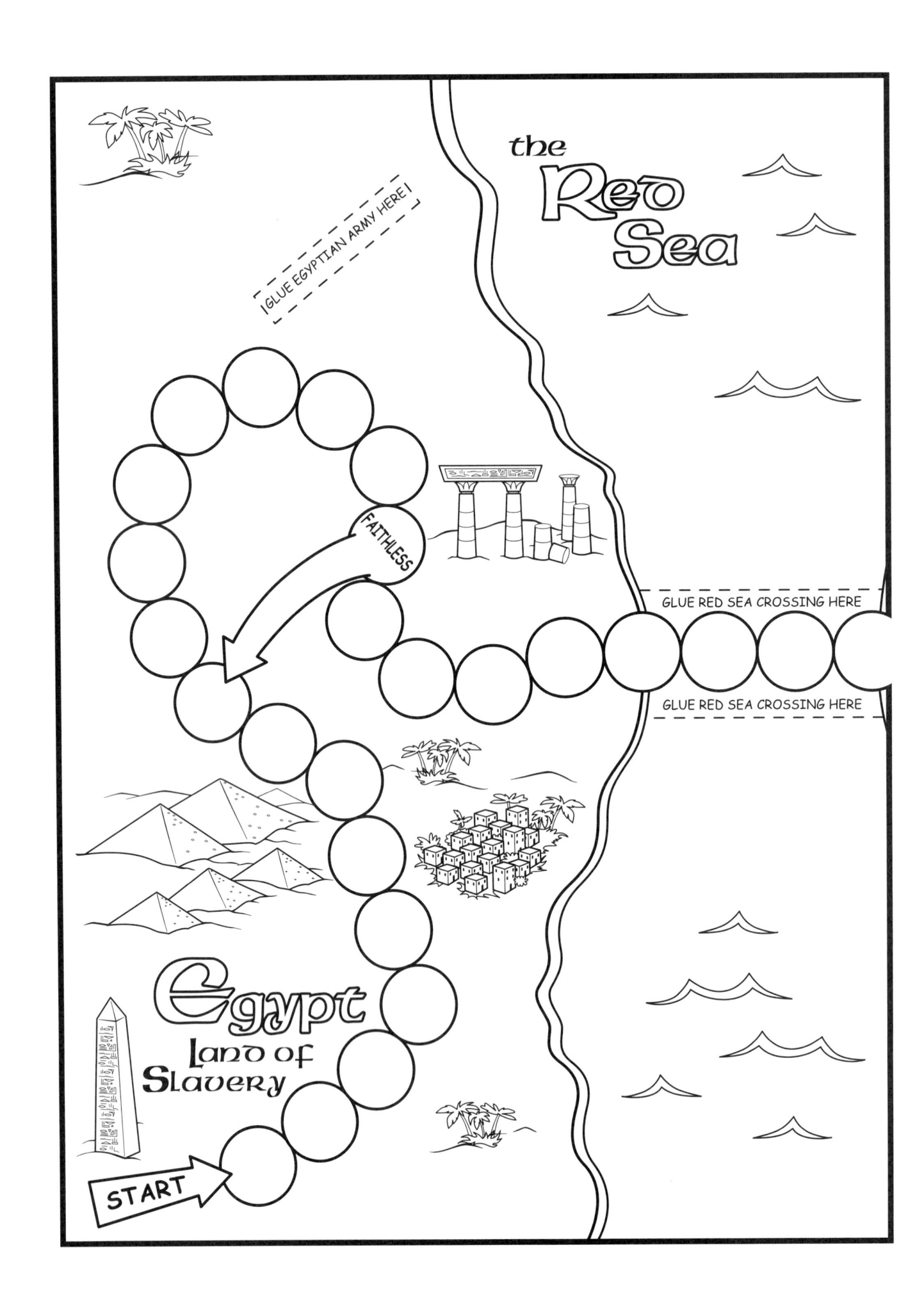

GLUE EGYPTIAN ARMY HERE

FAITHLESS

GLUE RED SEA CROSSING HERE

GLUE RED SEA CROSSING HERE

Egypt
Land of Slavery

START

GLUE TENT HERE

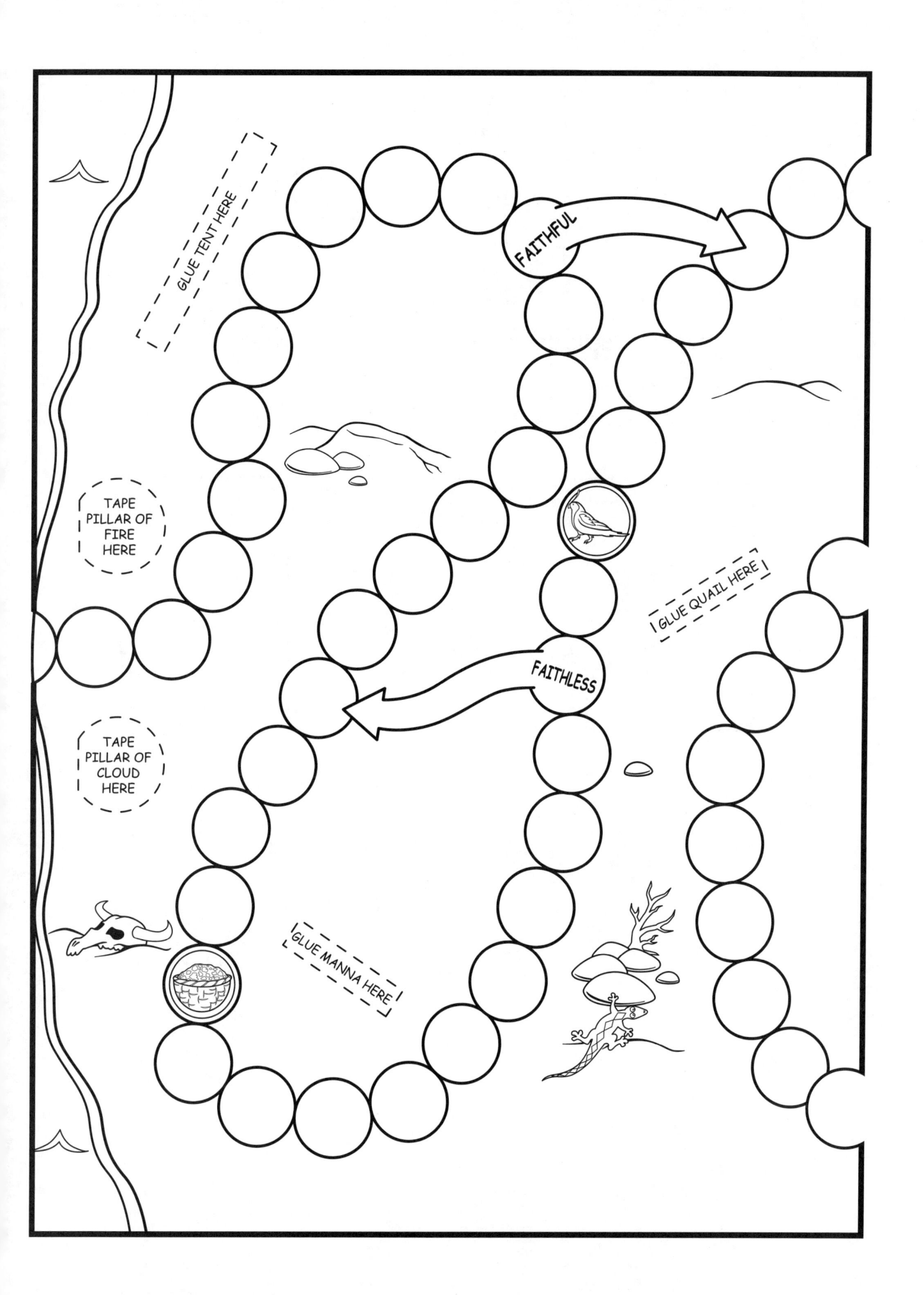

TAPE PILLAR OF FIRE HERE

TAPE PILLAR OF CLOUD HERE

FAITHFUL

GLUE QUAIL HERE

FAITHLESS

GLUE MANNA HERE

Panel 2. Glue to the middle left panel of the gameboard.

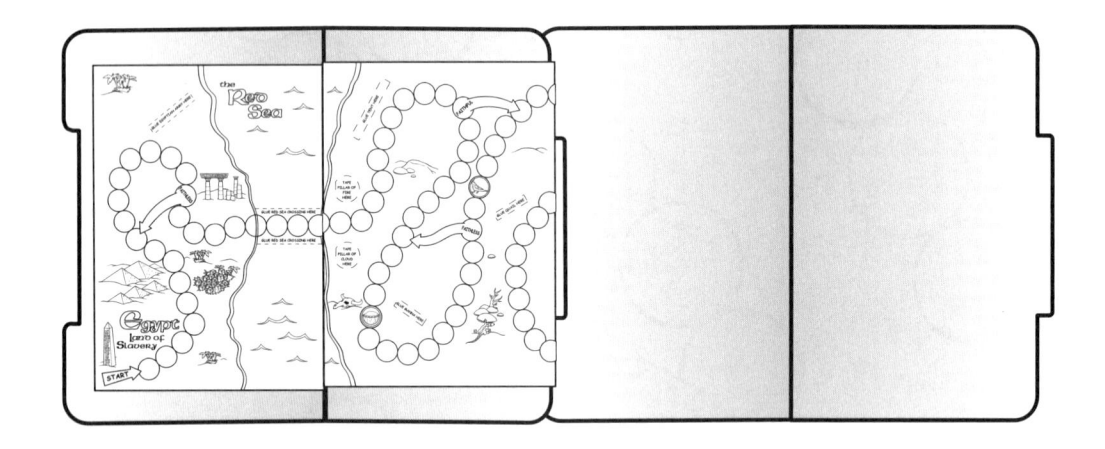

Panel 3. Glue to the middle right panel of the gameboard.

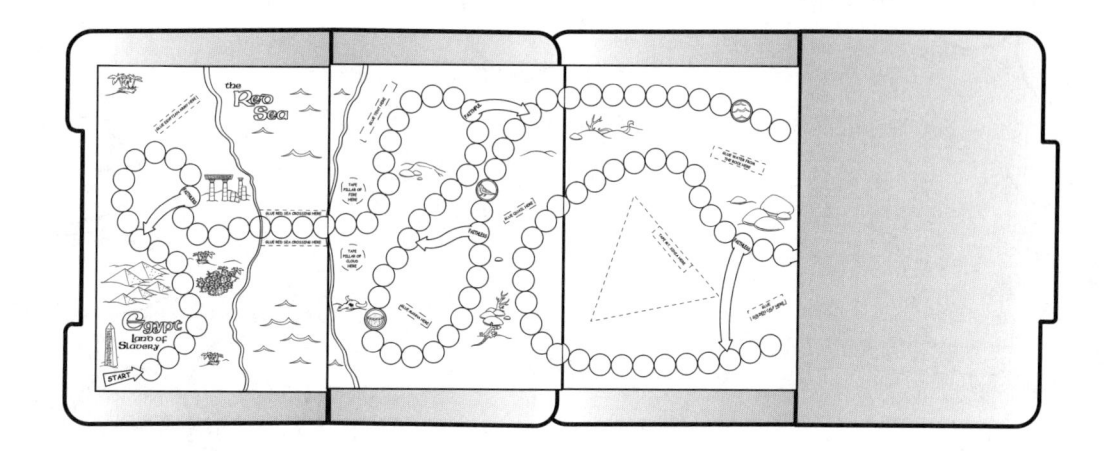

wanderin' the wilderness

GLUE WATER FROM THE ROCK HERE

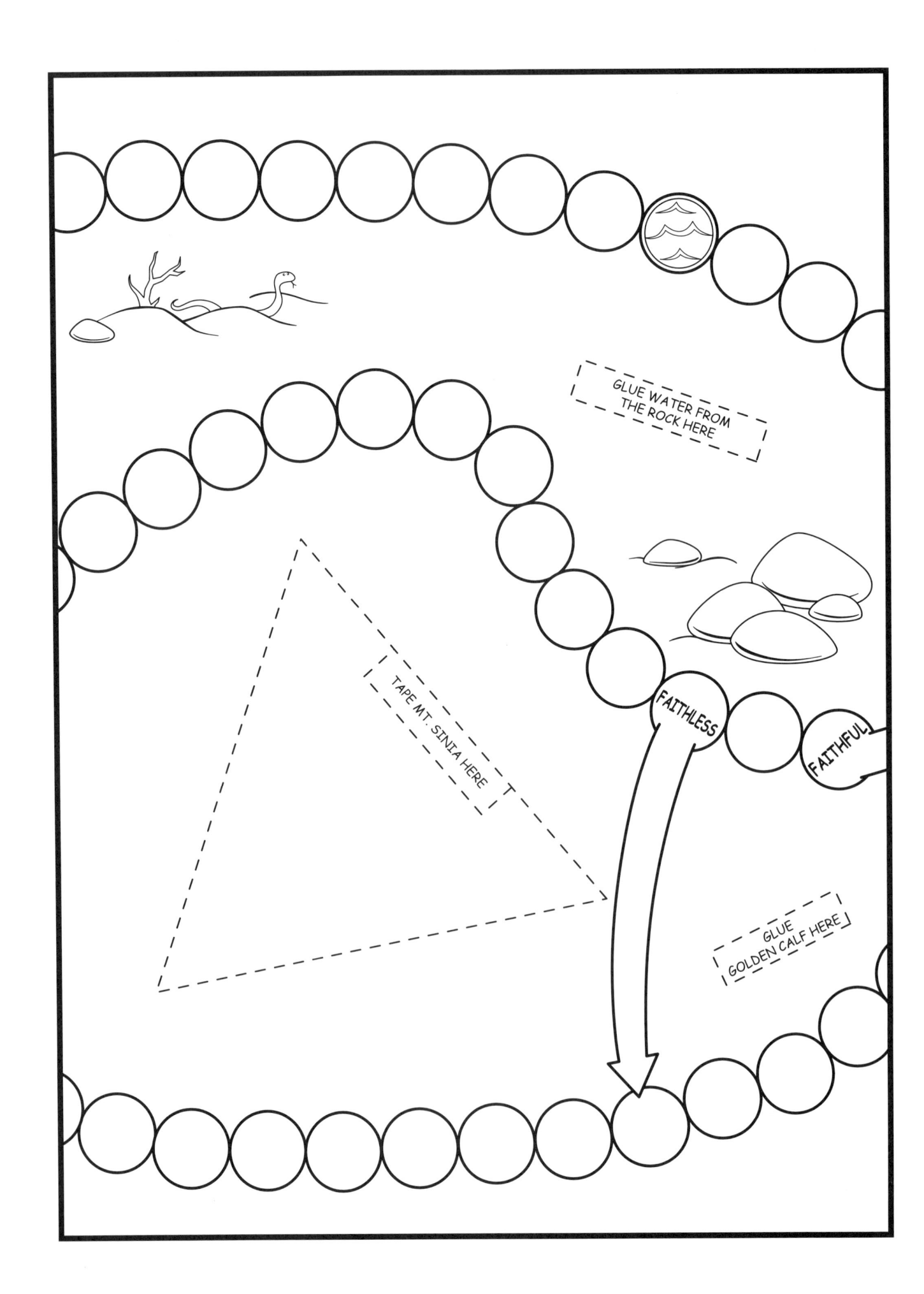

TAPE MT. SINIA HERE

FAITHLESS

FAITHFUL

GLUE GOLDEN CALF HERE

the Promised Land

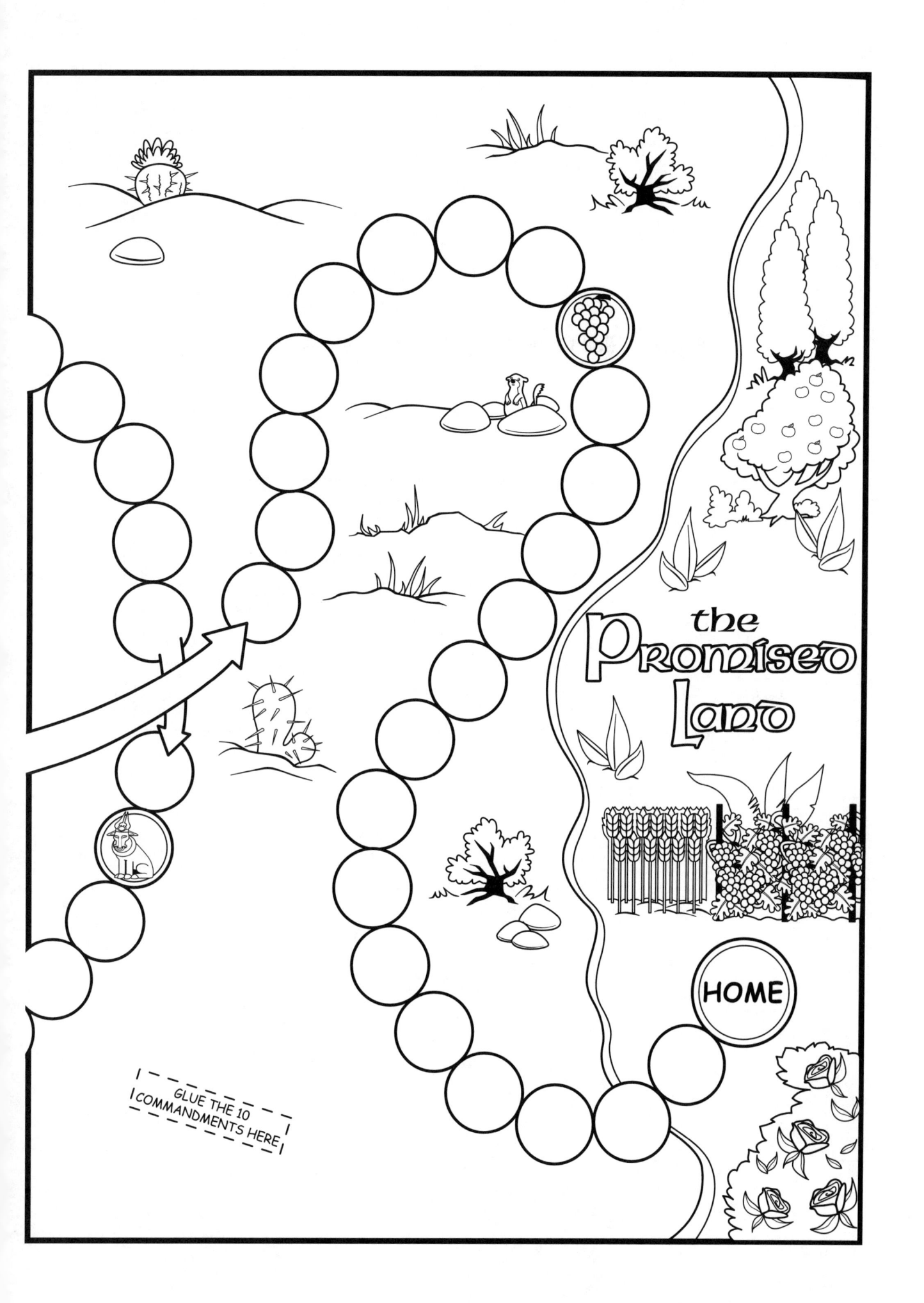

HOME

GLUE THE 10 COMMANDMENTS HERE

Panel 4. Glue to the far right panel of the gameboard.

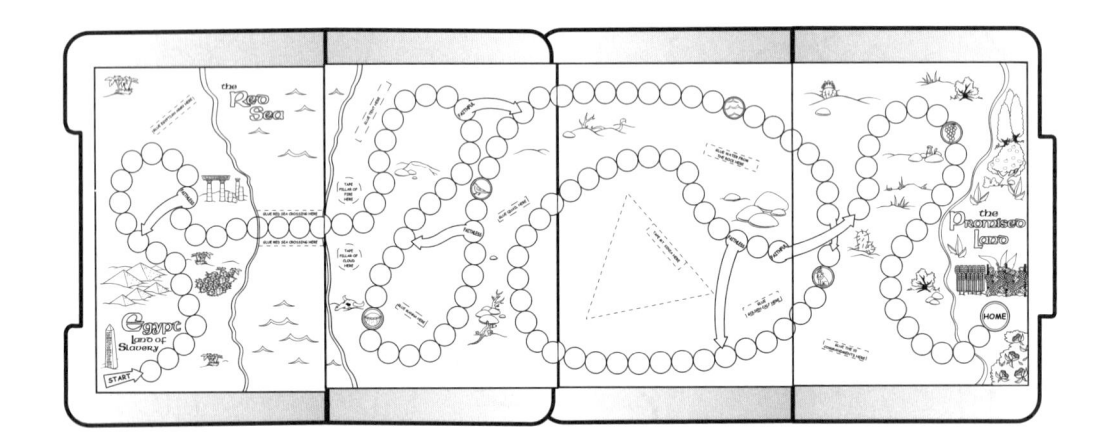

POP-UPS 1

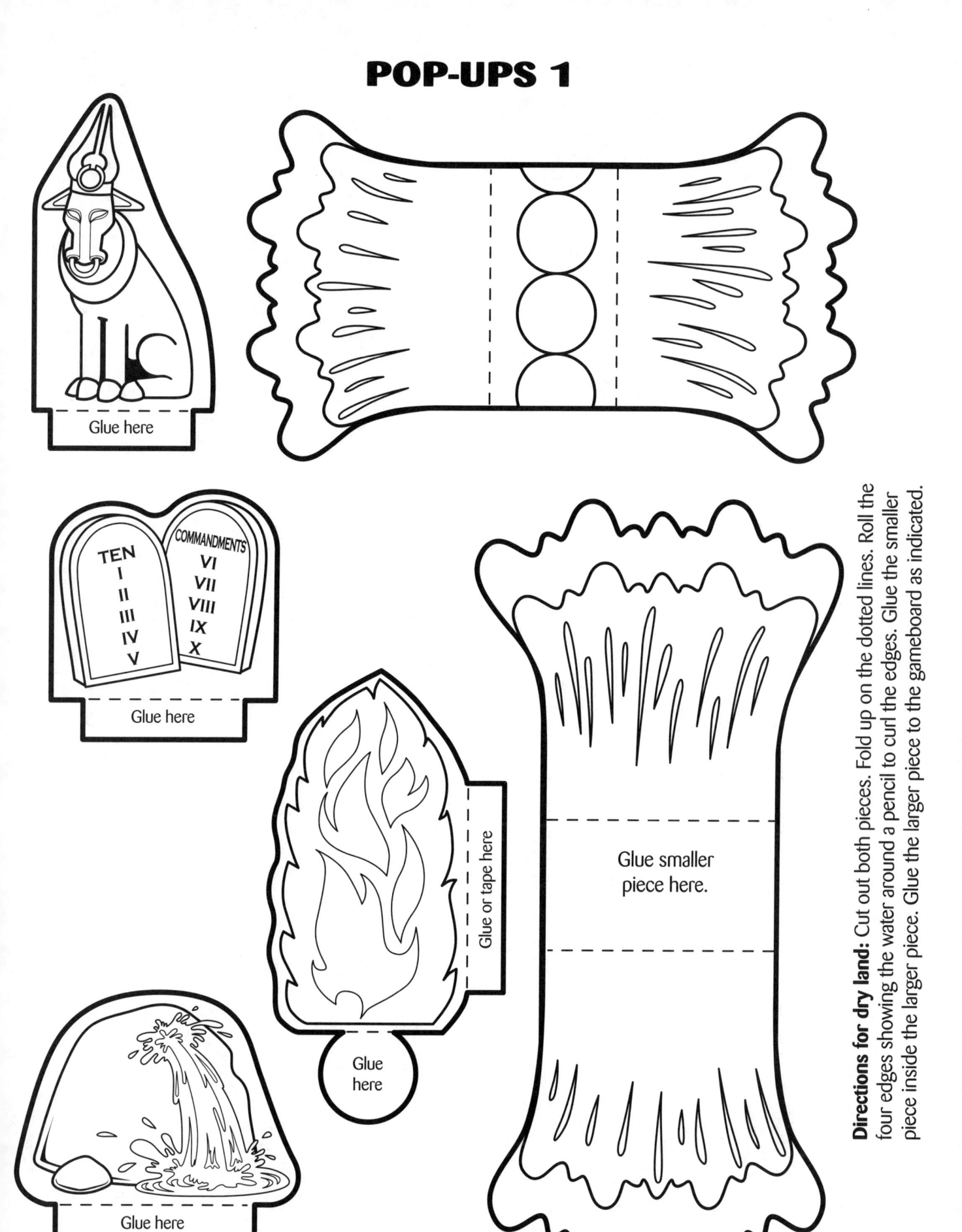

Glue here

Glue here

TEN COMMANDMENTS
I VI
II VII
III VIII
IV IX
V X

Glue here

Glue or tape here

Glue here

Glue smaller piece here.

Glue here

Directions for dry land: Cut out both pieces. Fold up on the dotted lines. Roll the four edges showing the water around a pencil to curl the edges. Glue the smaller piece inside the larger piece. Glue the larger piece to the gameboard as indicated.

wanderin' the wilderness 91

Glue inside larger piece.

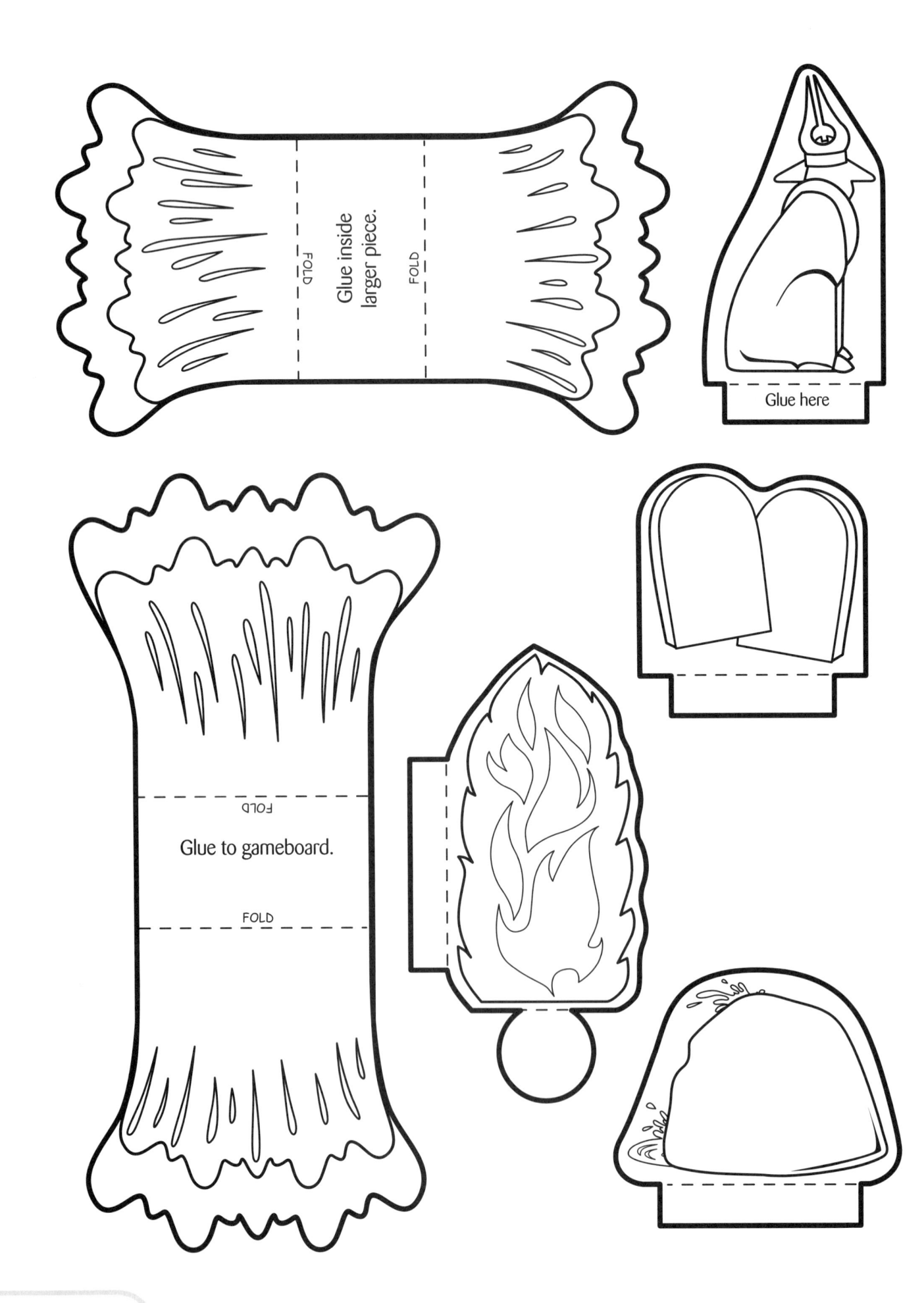

FOLD

FOLD

Glue here

FOLD

Glue to gameboard.

FOLD

92 folder games

POP-UPS 2

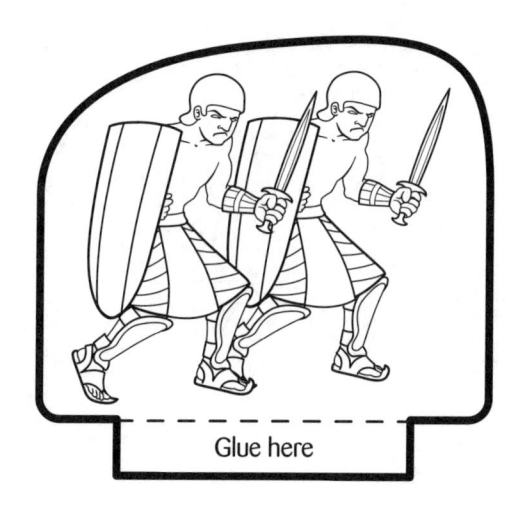

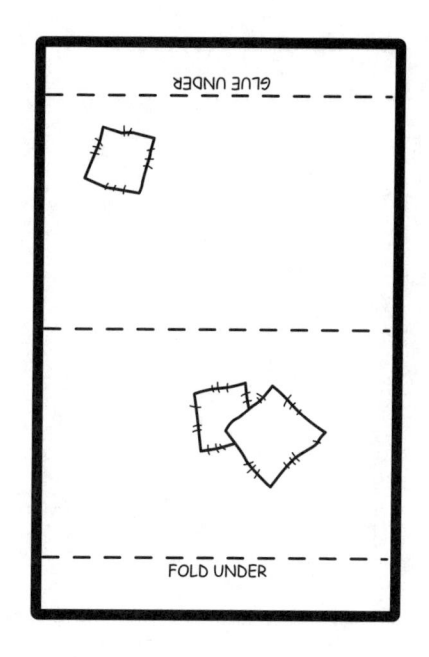

Glue here

Glue here

GLUE UNDER

FOLD UNDER

Glue here

Mt. Sinai directions: Cut out Mt. Sinai. Fold diagonally on the fold lines. Cut on the solid line until you get to the center mark. Overlaps the sections and glue the plain triangle underneath. Fold the "glue here" tab and glue to the gameboard.

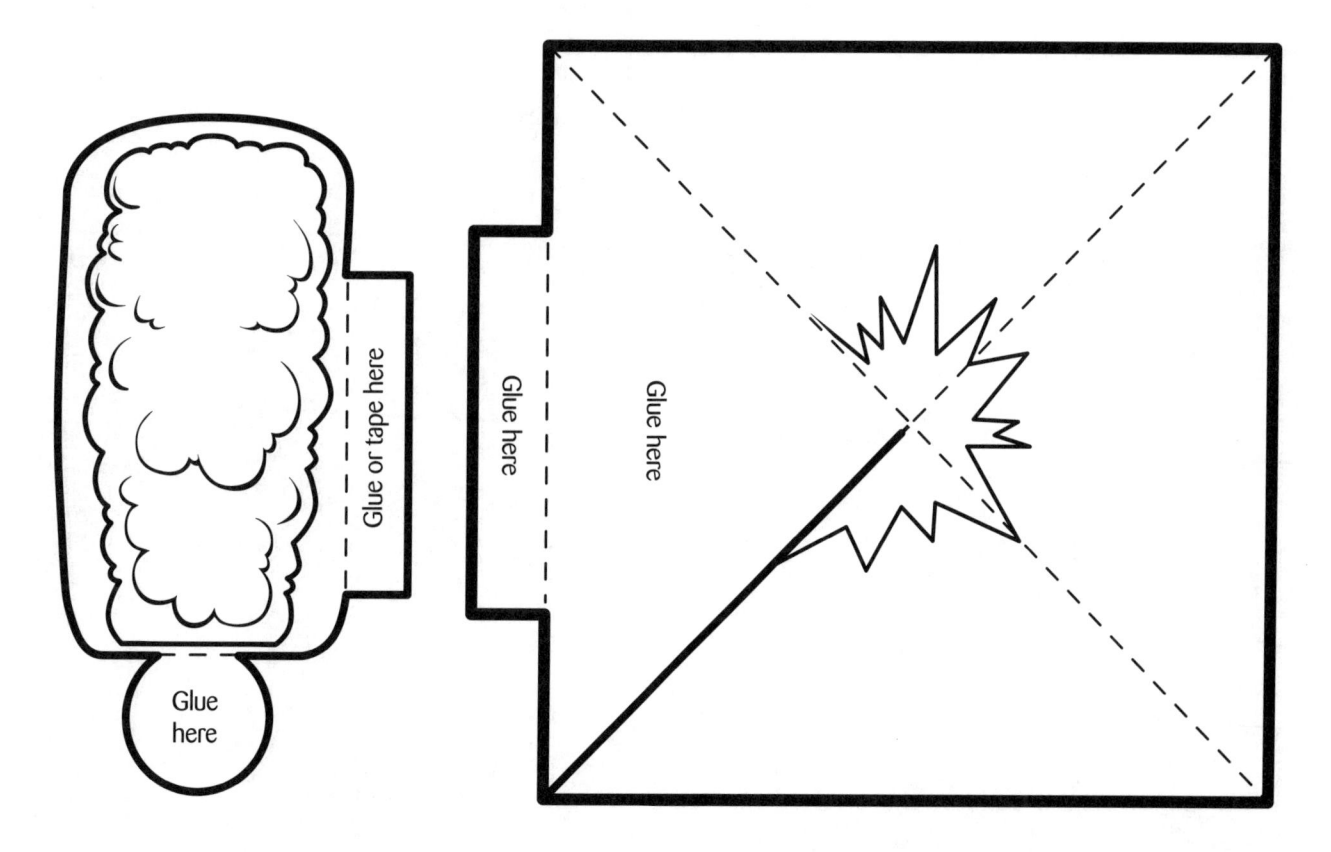

Glue or tape here

Glue here

Glue here

Glue here

wanderin' the wilderness

FOLD FOLD

FOLD

folder games

Whining and complaining!

Oh, no!
Go back
four spaces

Praising God!

You chose to praise God during hard times instead of whining.

Go ahead 4 spaces!

Who did God choose to lead the people?

A) Noah
B) Moses
C) Jonah

answer: B

Moses obeyed God when he helped lead the Israelites out of Egypt!

Name one way you can obey God today, then move 2 spaces ahead.

Moses' mother saved him from death by placing him in a...

A) Basket on the river
B) stroller on the street
C) blanket on the bed

answer: c

The Egyptian people used the Jewish people as...

A) paid workers
B) slaves

answer: B

How did God speak to Moses to tell him to lead the slaves out of Egypt?

A) through a sheep
B) through another shepherd
C) through a burning bush

answer: c

God gave Moses a helper. Moses' helper was...

A) Joshua
B) Elijah
C) Aaron

answer: C

Which one of these was not one of the plagues God sent on Egypt?

A) Fire
B) Flies
C) Frogs

answer: A

Who refused to let the slaves leave due to his stubborn heart?

A) Moses
B) Pharaoh
C) Aaron

answer: B

When the angel of death passed over Egypt, God's people were all celebrating...

A) Christmas
B) Hanukkah
C) Passover

answer: C

Pharaoh finally let the slaves leave Egypt after...

A) his first born son died
B) the river turned to blood
C) he kept getting flies in his mouth

answer: A

wanderin' the wilderness

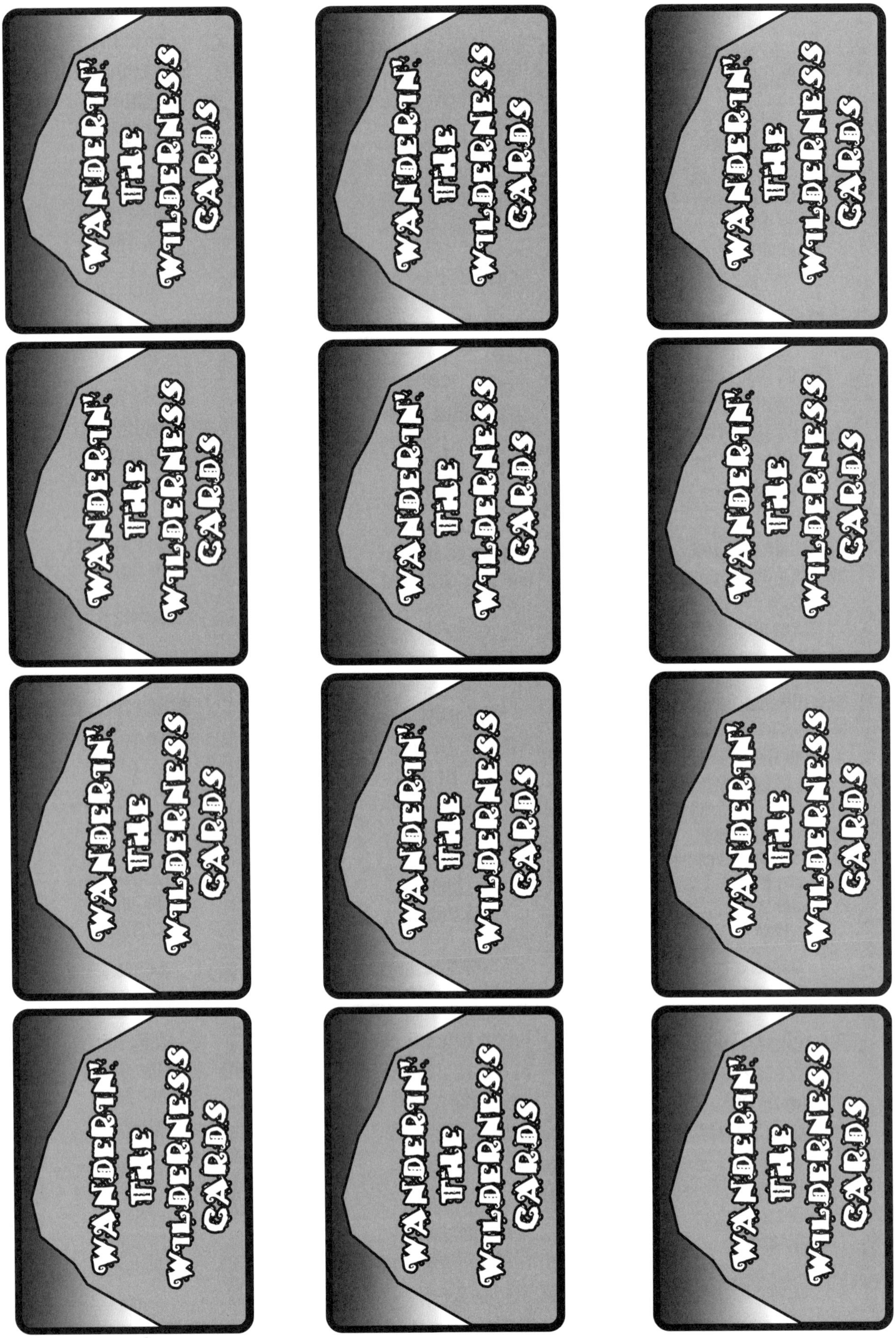
WANDERIN' THE WILDERNESS CARDS

Rotten Manna! Yuck!

You tried to save some manna for tomorrow and now it's rotten!

Go back 4 spaces!

Believing God Yippee!

You chose to believe that God would do the impossible.

Go ahead 4 spaces!

As the Jews were leaving, they asked the Egyptians for things. The Egyptians gave them...

A) nothing
B) gold, silver and clothing

answer: B

By day, the Lord went ahead of the Jews in a...

A) pillar of cloud
B) beautiful chariot
C) pillar of fire

answer: A

By night, the Lord led the people with a...

A) pillar of cloud
B) great big flashlight
C) pillar of fire

answer: C

Pharaoh's heart changed and he chased the Israelites. He caught up with them by...

A) Mount Sinai
B) the Mediterranean Ocean
C) the Red Sea

answer: C

The Lord saved his people from the Egyptians chasing them by...

A) parting the waters of the Red Sea
B) chasing the Egyptians away with the pillar of fire
C) burying the Egyptians in the sand.

answer: A

The Lord made sure the Jews had plenty to eat by providing what during the morning?

A) pancakes
B) manna
C) quails

answer: B

The Lord made sure the Jews had plenty to eat by providing what during the evening?

A) hamburgers
B) manna
C) quails

answer: C

If the people tried to save the manna for the next day, what would happen?

A) Nothing, they just saved themselves some work
B) It would disappear
C) It would become rotten

answer: C

The people became angry with Moses and demanded water. How did God provide the water?

A) Water cam out of the rock for the people
B) Moses found a well full of fresh water for the people
C) God caused it to rain

answer: A

God provided food, water, clothing and everything the Jews needed. What does God provide for you?

Answer, then move ahead 2 spaces.

wanderin' the wilderness

WANDERIN' THE WILDERNESS CARDS

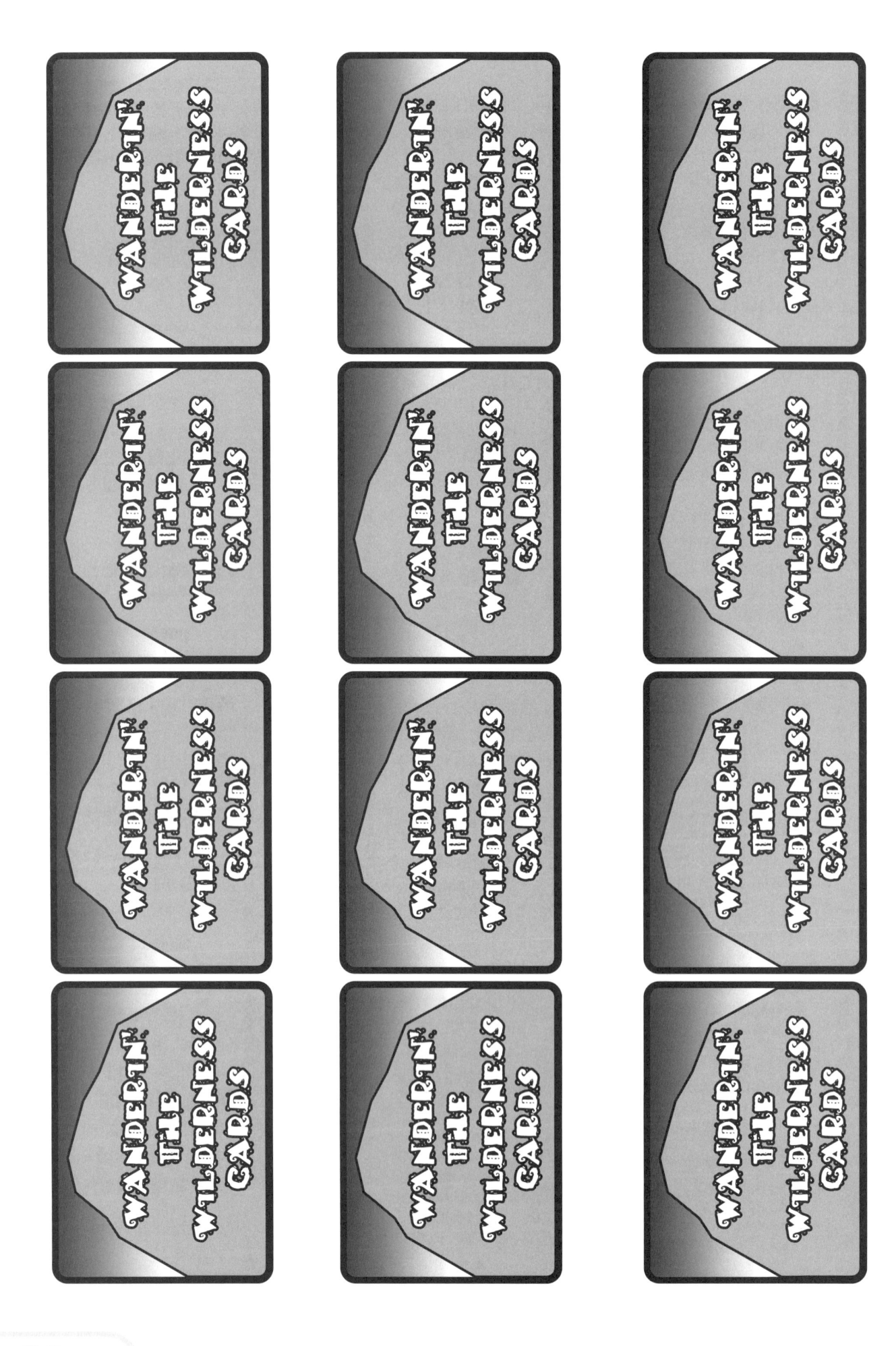

(12 card backs, each labeled "WANDERIN' THE WILDERNESS CARDS")

folder games

Card 1
Golden Calf!

Oh, no! You chose to worship the golden calf instead of God!

Go back 6 spaces!

Card 2
Following God!

Wow! You chose to follow God instead of man.

Go ahead 6 spaces!

Card 3
After three months of wandering, Moses went up on Mt. Sinai. What did God give Moses for the people?

A) More meat to eat
B) The Ten Commandments to follow
C) A new leader

answer: B

Card 4
Moses stayed up on Mt. Sinai for a long time. The people wanted to make a false God to worship. What did the people make?

A) a statue of Moses
B) a silver goat
C) a gold calf

answer: C

Card 5
When the people worshiped the golden calf, they disobeyed God.

Name one way people might disobey God today, then move ahead 2 spaces.

Card 6
Moses was angry when the people worshiped the calf, and he broke the stones with the Ten Commandments.

Name a good way to react when you're angry.

Answer, then move forward 2 spaces.

Card 7
When Moses came off of Mt. Sinai, his face was shining because...

A) he just washed it.
B) he had spoken with the Lord.
C) he was standing in the sunlight.

answer: B

Card 8
Moses and the people set up the holy tent for the Lord. On the day the tent was finished, what covered the tent?

A) a cloud
B) some rain
C) sunshine

answer: A

Card 9
What did the cloud that covered the holy tent look like at night?

A) a rainbow
B) still a cloud
C) fire

answer: C

Card 10
God's presence hovered over the holy tent.

Where does God live now?

Answer, then move ahead 2 spaces.

Card 11
The Jews had to wander in the wilderness for 40 years because they didn't trust God.

Share 1 thing you learned from this story, then move ahead 2 spaces.

Card 12
After 40 years, the Jews finally made it into the Promised Land. Who led them into that land?

A) Moses
B) Joshua
C) Elijah

answer: B

wanderin' the wilderness

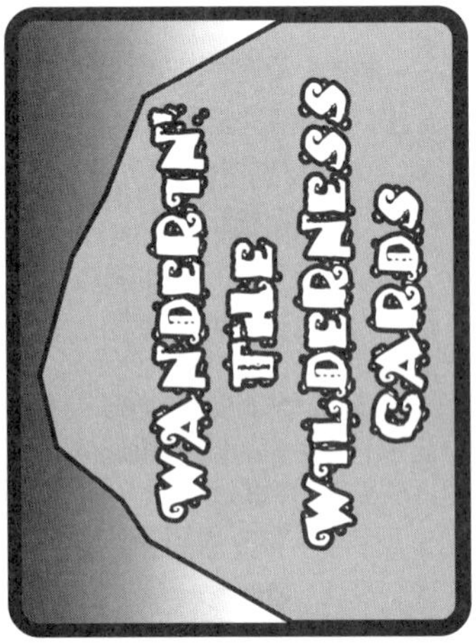
WANDERIN'
THE
WILDERNESS
CARDS
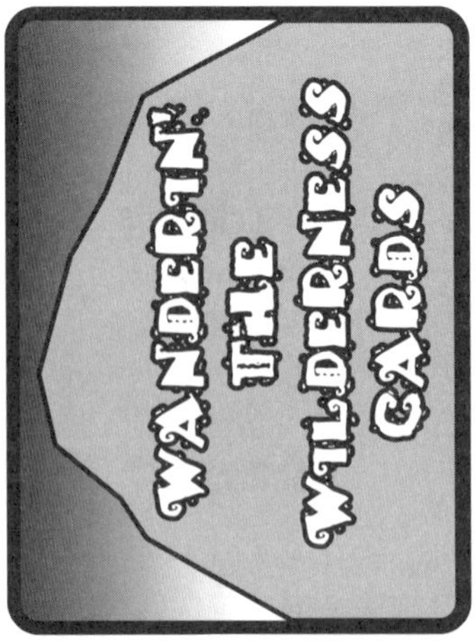
WANDERIN'
THE
WILDERNESS
CARDS
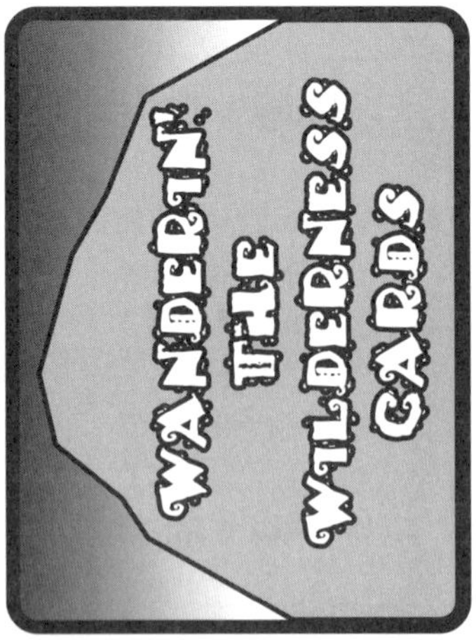
WANDERIN'
THE
WILDERNESS
CARDS
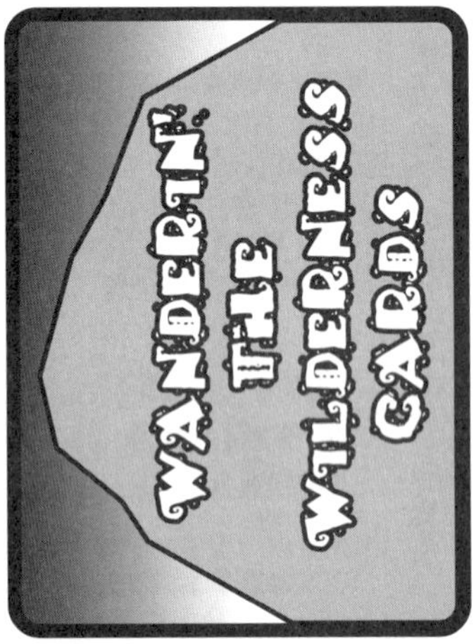
WANDERIN'
THE
WILDERNESS
CARDS
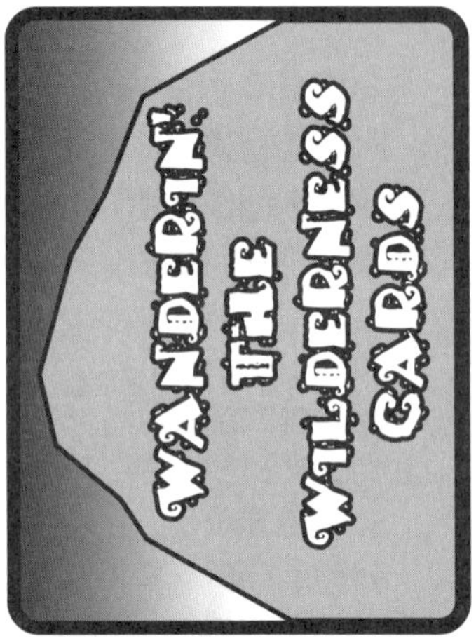
WANDERIN'
THE
WILDERNESS
CARDS
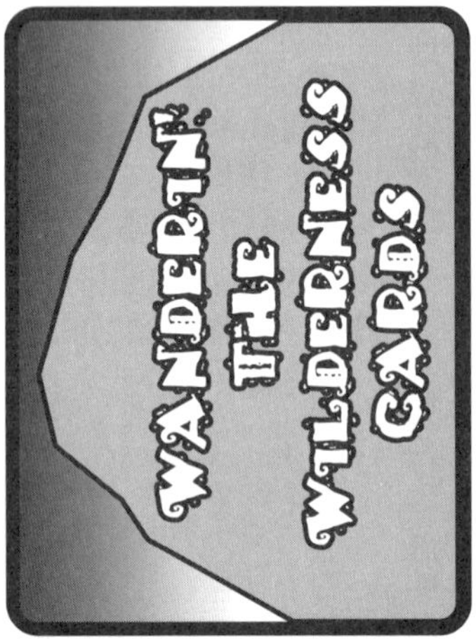
WANDERIN'
THE
WILDERNESS
CARDS
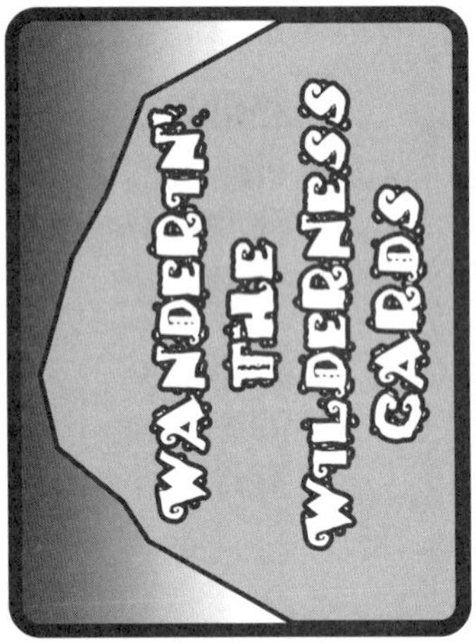
WANDERIN'
THE
WILDERNESS
CARDS
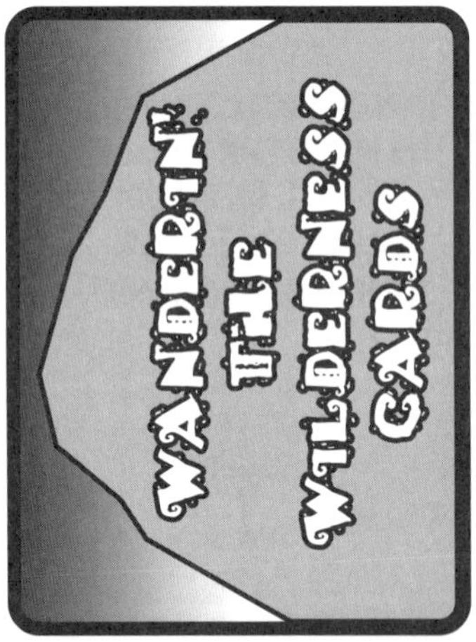
WANDERIN'
THE
WILDERNESS
CARDS
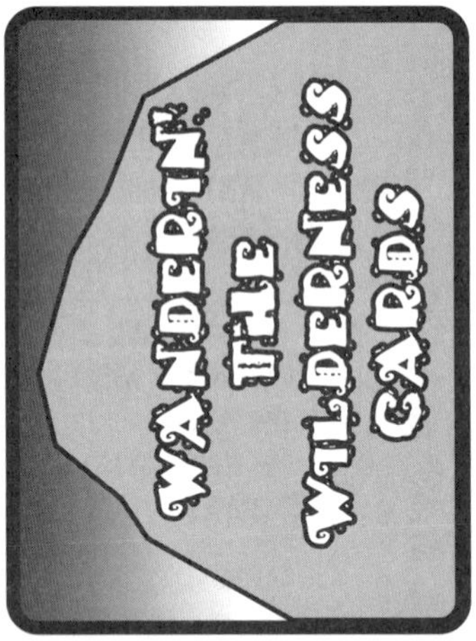
WANDERIN'
THE
WILDERNESS
CARDS
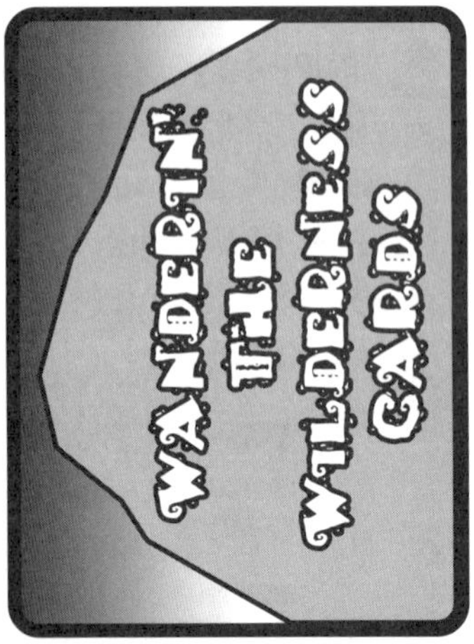
WANDERIN'
THE
WILDERNESS
CARDS
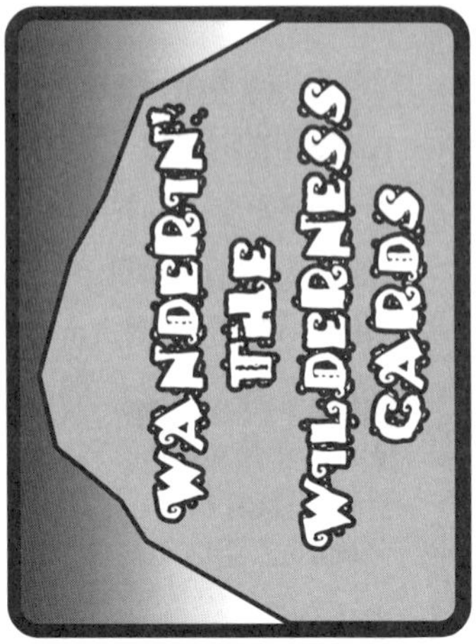
WANDERIN'
THE
WILDERNESS
CARDS
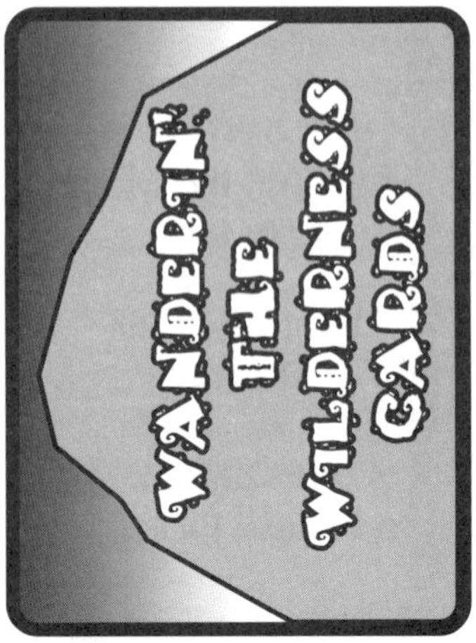
WANDERIN'
THE
WILDERNESS
CARDS

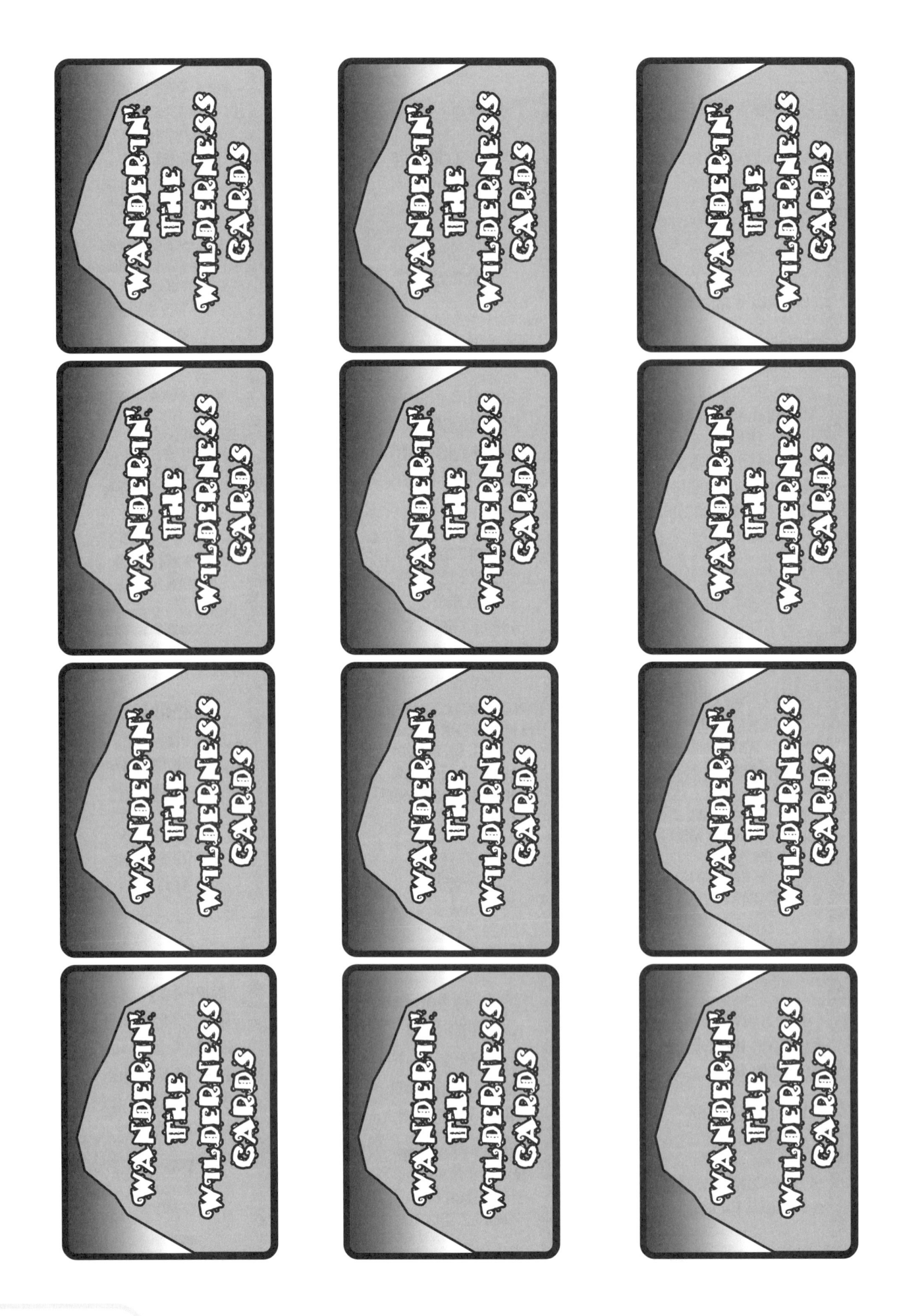

CHOICES! CHOICES!

Godprint: Integrity   Players: 2-6

Joseph and his brothers all faced many choices. They made some good ones, and some bad ones. We make choices, too. Play the fun game of Choices! Choices! to help you think about positive and negative choices.

Put It Together

1. Cut out the game title (above) and glue it to the front cover of a colorful folder.

2. Glue 'How to Play" (page 103) to the back of the folder. Leave room to glue an envelope or a zip-top bag above the rules in which you can store the game cards, game markers and coin.

3. Glue page 106 to the inside left of the folder. Glue page 107 to the inside right of the folder. Add color as desired.

4. Cut apart the "Move!" cards (page 109) and the "Choose!" cards (pages 109, 111 and 113).

5. Color 6 wagon-wheel pastas with different colored markers to use as fun game pieces.

GET LIST:
- colorful folder
- glue stick and scissors
- markers or colored pencils
- envelope or zip-top bag
- 6 wagon-wheel pasta
- permanent markers
- quarter or other large two-sided coin

choices! choices!

Glue to front of game folder.

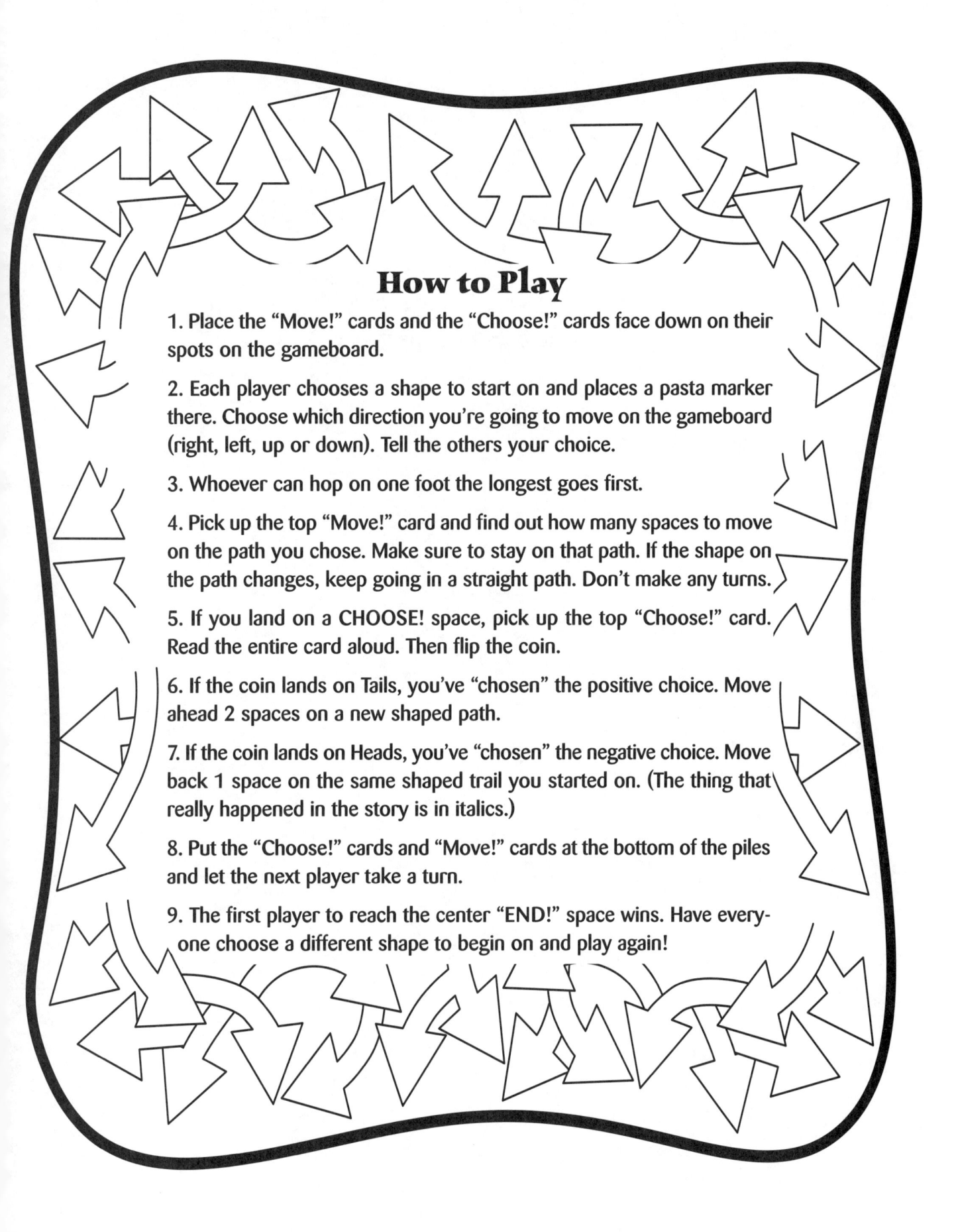

How to Play

1. Place the "Move!" cards and the "Choose!" cards face down on their spots on the gameboard.

2. Each player chooses a shape to start on and places a pasta marker there. Choose which direction you're going to move on the gameboard (right, left, up or down). Tell the others your choice.

3. Whoever can hop on one foot the longest goes first.

4. Pick up the top "Move!" card and find out how many spaces to move on the path you chose. Make sure to stay on that path. If the shape on the path changes, keep going in a straight path. Don't make any turns.

5. If you land on a CHOOSE! space, pick up the top "Choose!" card. Read the entire card aloud. Then flip the coin.

6. If the coin lands on Tails, you've "chosen" the positive choice. Move ahead 2 spaces on a new shaped path.

7. If the coin lands on Heads, you've "chosen" the negative choice. Move back 1 space on the same shaped trail you started on. (The thing that really happened in the story is in italics.)

8. Put the "Choose!" cards and "Move!" cards at the bottom of the piles and let the next player take a turn.

9. The first player to reach the center "END!" space wins. Have everyone choose a different shape to begin on and play again!

Glue to back of game folder.

Panel 1. Glue to the inside left of the game folder.

START

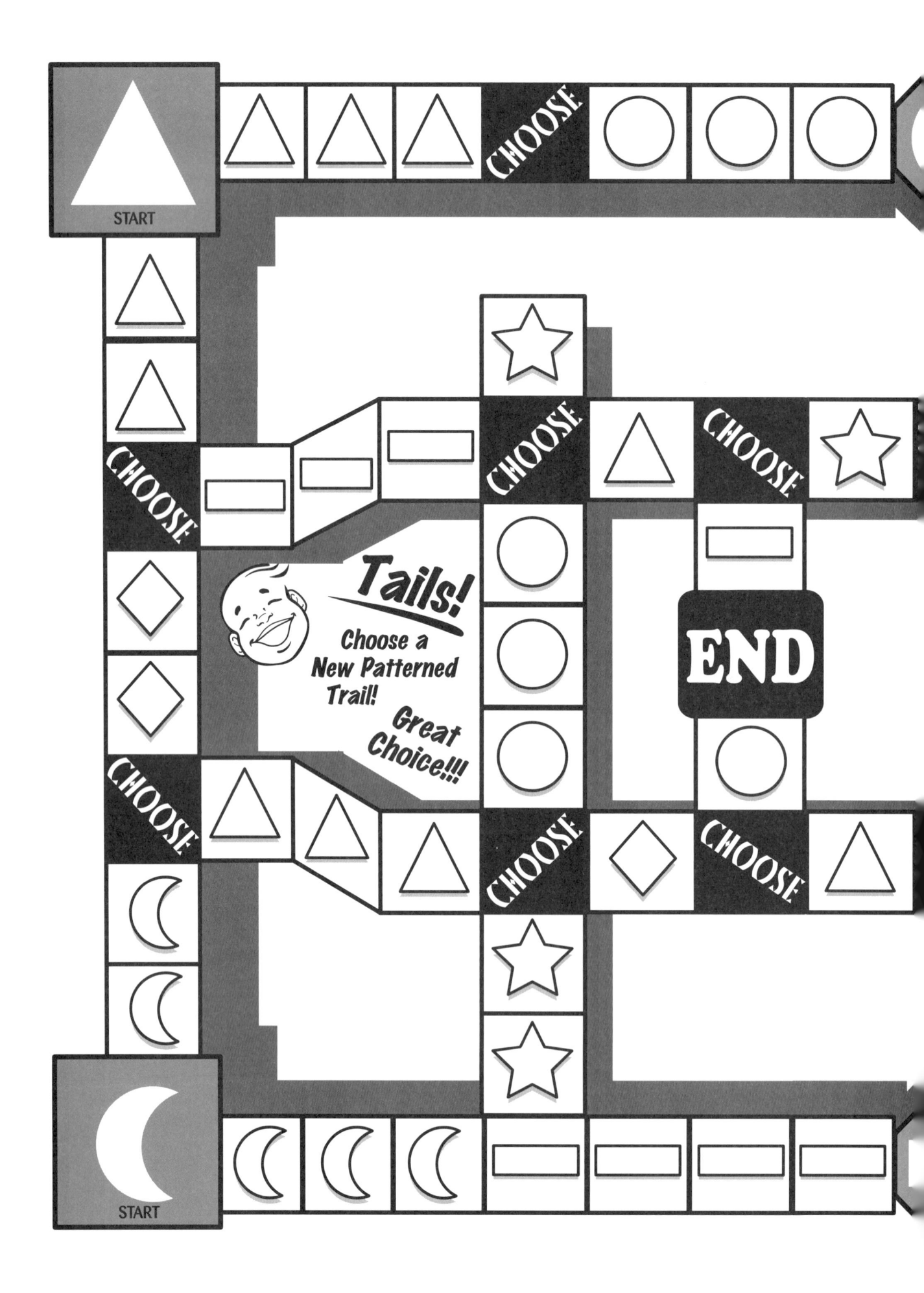

CHOOSE

Tails! Choose a New Patterned Trail! Great Choice!!!

CHOOSE

CHOOSE

CHOOSE

END

CHOOSE

CHOOSE

START

START

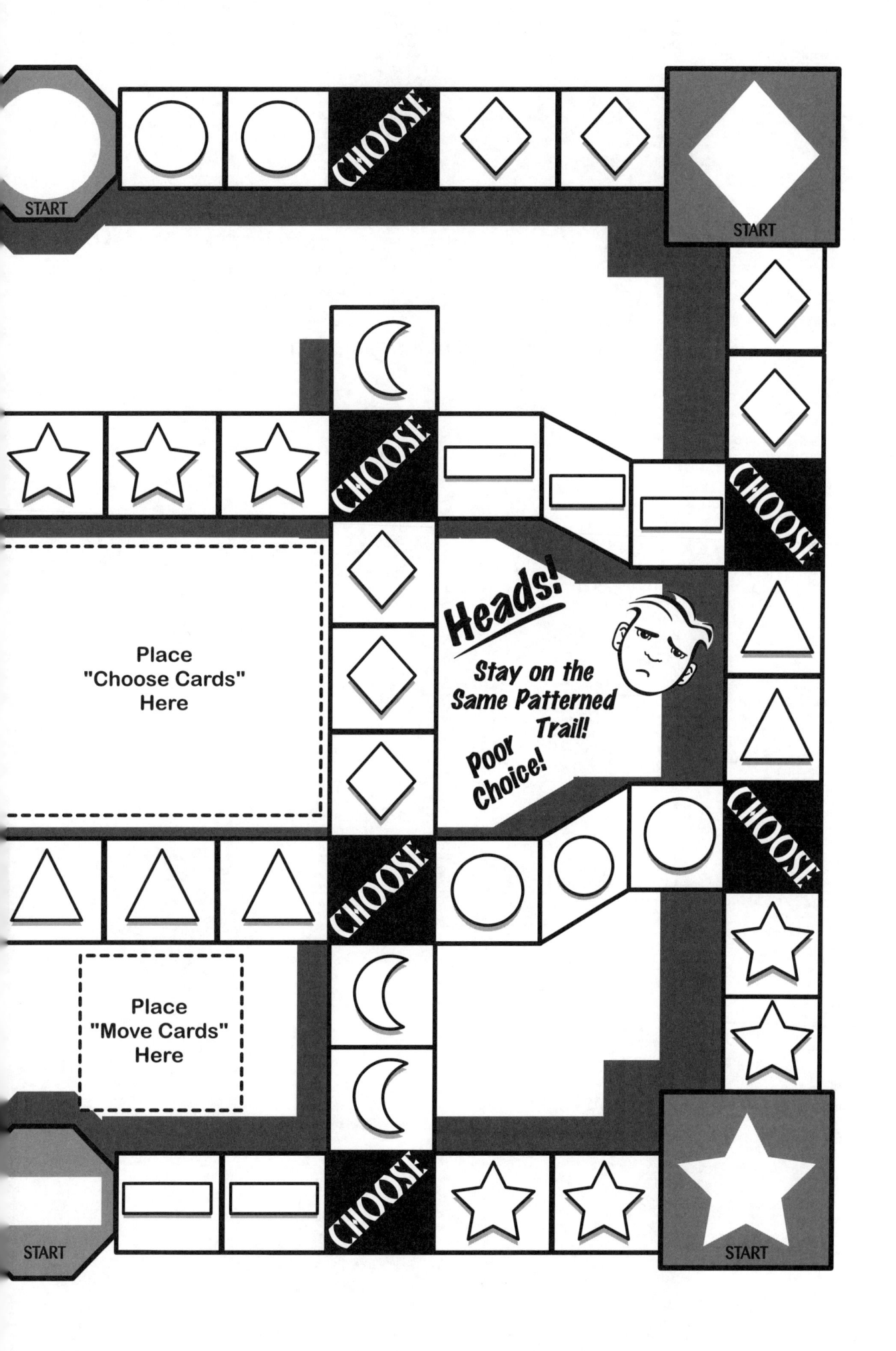

CHOOSE

START

Place "Choose Cards" Here

Heads!
Stay on the Same Patterned Trail!
Poor Choice!

CHOOSE

CHOOSE

Place "Move Cards" Here

CHOOSE

START

CHOOSE

START

Glue to the inside right of the game folder.

1	2	3	4	1	2
3	4	1	2	3	4
1	2	3	4	1	2
3	4	1	2	3	4

Jacob had 12 sons. Joseph was his favorite son because he was a child of Jacob's old age. Jacob gave Joseph a beautiful coat made of many colors.

Tails: Joseph thanked his father for the special gift.
Heads: Joseph said he didn't like it and never wore the gift.

Jacob sent Joseph to check on his brothers in the field with the sheep. The brothers were not doing their job properly.

Tails: Joseph told his father the truth.
Heads: Joseph lied to protect his brothers from punishment.

Jacob's sons saw that Jacob loved Joseph the most.

Tails: They were happy that Joseph was their father's favorite.
Heads: They were jealous of Joseph and treated him badly.

God gave Joseph dreams about his future. Joseph told his family about the dreams.

Tails: His family rejoiced with Joseph over the dreams.
Heads: His family became more jealous of Joseph.

Jacob sent Joseph to his brothers working in the field. They saw Joseph a long way off.

Tails: They decided to make enough dinner so Joseph could eat with them.
Heads: They decided to kill Joseph.

Rueben, one of Joseph's brothers, told his brothers:

Tails: "Let's not actually kill Joseph."
Heads: "Let's kill him right away."

choices! choices!

When Joseph arrived in the field where his brothers were, they saw he was wearing his special, colorful coat.

Tails: The brothers told Joseph how nice he looked in his new coat.
Heads: The brothers took the coat away from Joseph.

The brothers found an old well that didn't have any water in it.

Tails: They looked around for a well with some water so they could drink.
Heads: They threw Joseph in the old, dry well.

As the brothers were eating, some traders going to Egypt came by.

Tails: The brothers traded for some rope to get Joseph out of the well.
Heads: The brothers sold Joseph to the traders for some silver.

Rueben saw that the other brothers sold Joseph.

Tails: He tore his clothes in grief and told his father the truth.
Heads: He tore his clothes in grief and didn't tell his father the truth.

The brothers had to explain to their father about Joseph's disappearance.

Tails: They told their father the truth.
Heads: They lied to their father and said an animal attacked Joseph.

Joseph became a slave for an Egyptian ruler named Potiphar.

Tails: Joseph worked very well for his new master.
Heads: Joseph did as little work as possible.

Potiphar was very pleased with Joseph's work.

Tails: Potiphar told Joseph how pleased he was with his work and gave Joseph the best job in his household.
Heads: Potiphar didn't tell Joseph how pleased he was with him.

Potiphar's wife wanted Joseph to do something he knew was wrong.

Tails: Joseph refused because it was wrong.
Heads: Joseph said "Okay" and snuck around so Potiphar wouldn't know.

Since Joseph refused to do what Potiphar's wife wanted…

Tails: She respected him and left him alone.
Heads: She became angry and lied about Joseph.

When Potiphar heard the lie his wife told…

Tails: He got Joseph out of trouble.
Heads: He put Joseph in prison.

Joseph worked very hard in prison. He always did his best for the prison master.

Tails: The prison master put Joseph in charge of many duties to honor Joseph.
Heads: The prison master punished Joseph for working so hard.

Two of Pharaoh's workers were sent to prison. God gave each of them a dream.

Tails: Joseph told the men what their dreams meant.
Heads: Joseph ignored the men, refusing to even speak to them.

choices! choices!

folder games

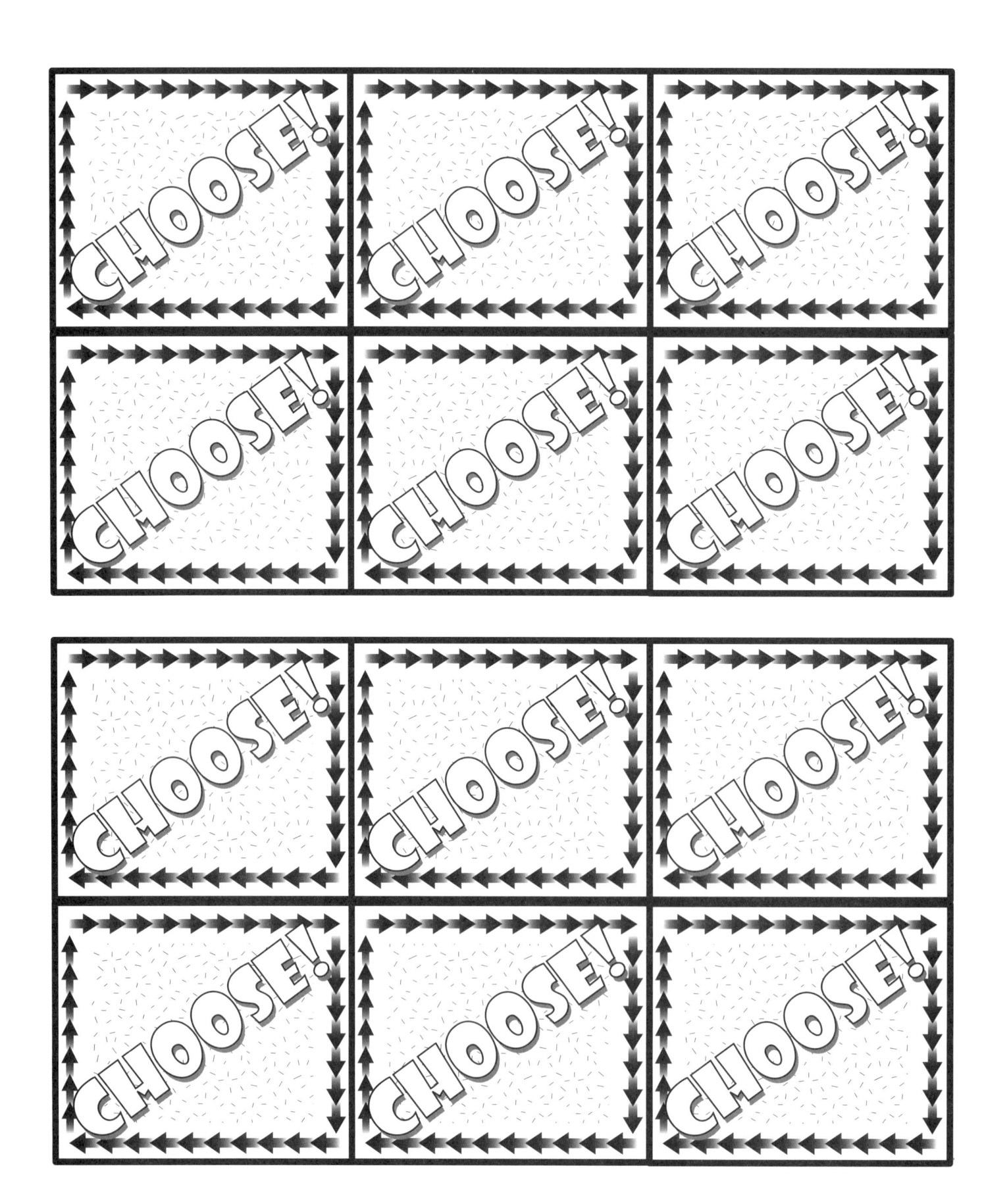

Joseph asked Pharaoh's workers to speak to Pharaoh about him so that he could get out of prison. When one of the men went back to work he…

Tails: immediately told Pharaoh about Joseph.
Heads: forgot about Joseph and just went back to work.

Later, God gave Pharaoh two dreams. No one could tell Pharaoh what the dreams meant. The worker who once was in prison remembered Joseph.

Tails: The worker told Pharaoh about the man who could interpret dreams.
Heads: The worker said nothing to Pharaoh so he wouldn't get in trouble.

Pharaoh called for Joseph to tell him what his dreams meant.

Tails: Joseph told Pharaoh what both dreams meant.
Heads: Joseph was so angry for being thrown in jail for no reason that he refused to speak to Pharaoh.

Pharaoh was so pleased with Joseph that he…

Tails: made Joseph second in charge of all of Egypt.
Heads: threw Joseph back in prison.

Joseph began to work for Pharaoh.

Tails: He worked his hardest to save up enough food for all the people in a famine.
Heads: Joseph was just glad to get out of prison and didn't do anything.

The famine came. People from countries all around came to Egypt to buy food.

Tails: Joseph gladly sold food to anyone who needed it.
Heads: Joseph said the food was only for the Egyptians.

One day Joseph's brothers came to buy food.

Tails: Joseph gave his brothers food.
Heads: To pay them back for selling him as a slave, Joseph refused to give them any food.

Joseph saw that his brothers were sorry for what they had done. He told them who he was.

Tails: Joseph forgave his brothers for what they had done.
Heads: Joseph refused to forgive his brothers and put them all in prison.

Joseph sent his brothers back to his father. He wanted his father to…

Tails: bring all his people to Egypt where there was plenty of food for everyone.
Heads: punish his brothers for what they'd done to him.

Sometimes people do bad things to us, as Joseph's brothers did to him. What should we do then?

Tails: Forgive them.
Heads: Be mean right back.

What would you do if you were punished at school for something you didn't do?

Tails: Remember that God knows the truth and still do your best.
Heads: Throw a tantrum and refuse to do any of your work.

Sometimes others get things we want, such as when Joseph got the coat of many colors but his brothers didn't. How should we react?

Tails: Be happy for them.
Heads: Be jealous.

choices! choices!

folder games

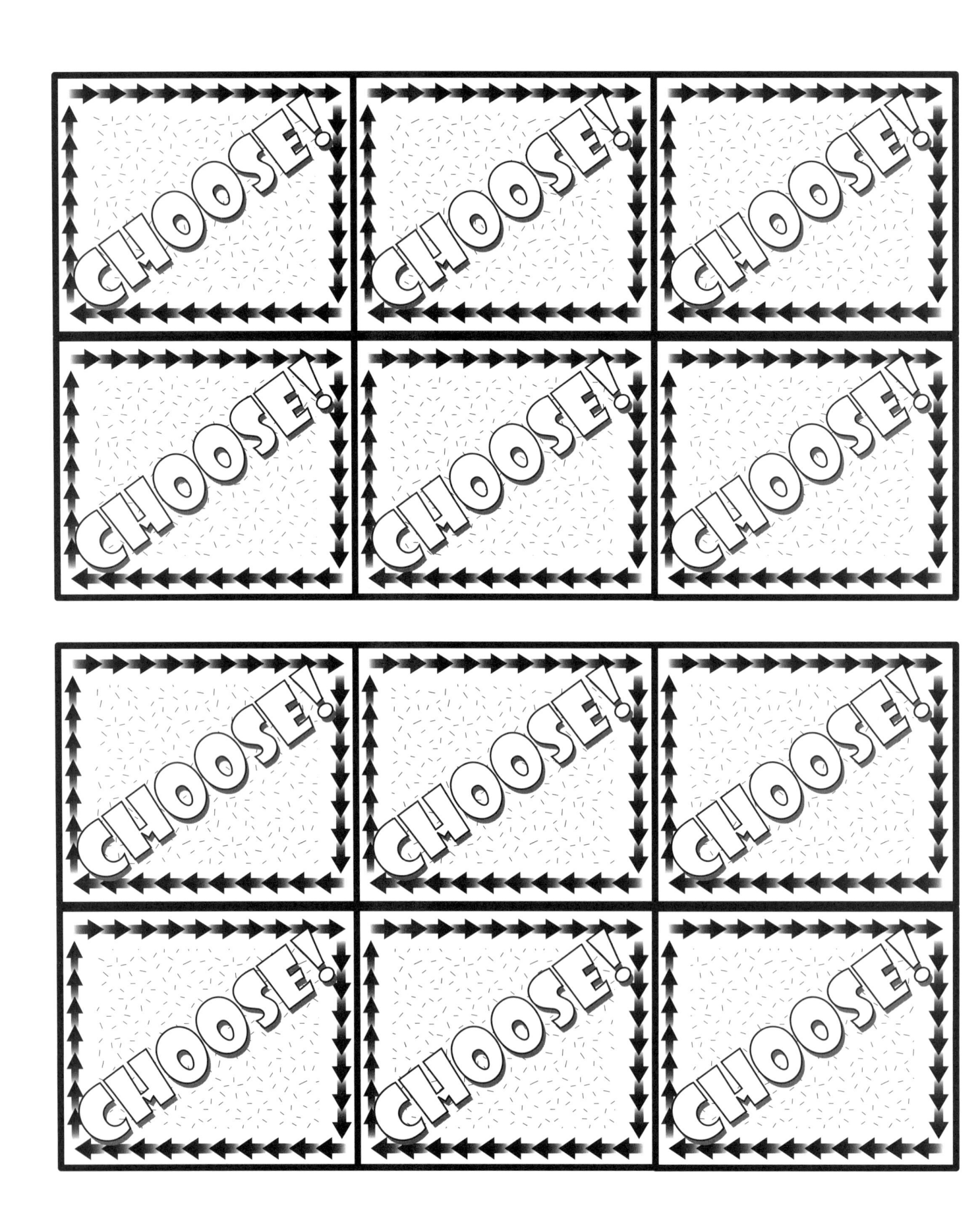

BIFF or BALANCE

Godprint: Thankfulness   Players: 6 or more

John wrote about Jesus so that we would know that God loves us enough to send Jesus to live on earth and die for us. Have a movin' good time as you show what you remember about Jesus from the Gospel of John.

Put It Together

1. Glue the game's title (above) to the front cover of a colorful folder.

2. Glue "How to Play" (page 117) to the back of the folder. Leave room to glue an envelope or a zip-top bag above the rules in which you can store the game cards.

3. Glue page 120 to the inside left side of the folder. Glue page 121 to the inside right side of the folder. Make sure the balance beam lines up correctly before you glue the pages to the folder. Add color as desired.

4. Cut apart the "Biff" or "Balance" cards (pages 123, 125 and 127).

GET LIST:
- colorful file folder
- scissors
- glue stick
- envelope or zip-top bag

Optional:
- crayons or markers

biff or balance

Glue to front of game folder.

How to Play

GET LIST: ♦ a referee

1. Count off by twos to form teams. Gather one team on each side of the gameboard and take off your shoes. Line up your team in order of height. Put the tallest person in the front.

2. The first player from each team steps up to the gameboard. Put your toes on the toe outline. Press the palms of your hands against your opponent's hands about shoulder height.

3. When the players are ready, the referee says, "Go!" Keep your palms flat against your opponent's hands and press hard. Try to make the other player step off the gameboard.

4. When one of the players moves a foot off the gameboard, the referee calls "Biff!" Then the referee draws a question card and reads it to the player who "Balanced" and is still standing on the game board. If the player answers correctly, that team gets 5 points. The referee keeps score. If the "Balance" player can't answer the question, the "Biff" player gets a chance. If the Biff player answers correctly, that team gets 4 points.

5. If the "Biff" player can't answer the question, the "Balance" team gets a chance. If they answer correctly, they get 3 points. If not, the "Biff" team gets a chance. If they answer correctly, they get 2 points.

6. Once the question is answered, the next player on each team steps up to the gameboard.

7. The first team to reach 50 points wins.

Glue to back of the game folder.

Glue to the inside left of the gameboard.

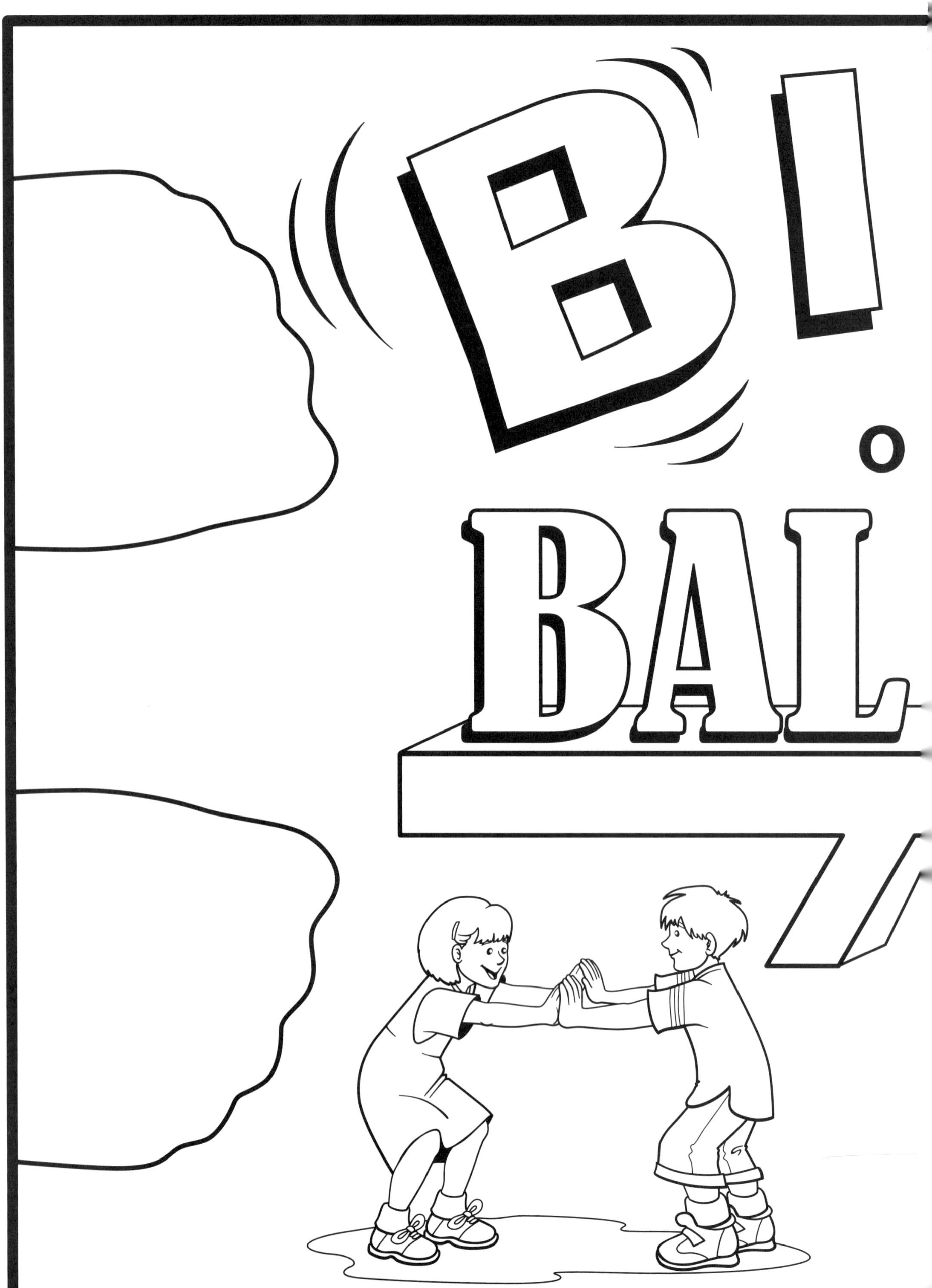
B!
o
BAL

FF
r
ANCE

Glue to the inside right of the game folder.

Q: What town did Jesus come from?

A: Nazareth. (John 1:45)

Q: What new command did Jesus give his disciples?

A: Love one another as I have loved you. (John 13:34)

Q: Who poured expensive perfume on Jesus?

A: Mary. (John 12:3)

Q: What food did Jesus say he was?

A: Bread of life. (John 6:35)

Q: What animal caretaker did Jesus call himself?

A: The good shepherd. (John 10:11)

Q: What was Jesus' first miracle?

A: He turned water to wine at a wedding at Cana. (John 2:1–11)

Q: Where did Jesus overturn tables?

A: At the temple. (John 2:12–23)

Q: Finish this sentence three ways. Jesus said, "I am the…"

A: (any 3) bread of life, light of the world, resurrection and the life, good shepherd, gate for the sheep, way the truth and the life, true vine. (John 6:48; 8:12; 10:7, 9, 11, 14; 14:6; 15:1.)

Q: Who was the Roman ruler who handed Jesus over to be crucified?

A: Pilate. (John 19:16)

Q: Who was the first person to find the empty tomb?

A: Mary Magdalene. (John 20:1)

folder games

Q: A Pharisee came to talk to Jesus by night. Who was he?

A: Nicodemus. (John 3:1)

Q: What did John the Baptist call Jesus when he saw him coming?

A: The Lamb of God. (John 1:29, 1:35)

Q: What did John the Baptist baptize with?

A: Water. (John 1:26)

Q: How did the Holy Spirit show himself at Jesus' baptism?

A: As a dove. (John 1:32)

Q: The first two disciples Jesus called were Simon Peter and his brother…

A: Andrew. (John 1:40–42)

Q: What did the people say when Jesus rode into Jerusalem on a donkey?

A: Hosanna! (John 12:12–14)

Q: Finish these words of Jesus: "Destroy this temple and…"

A: I will raise it again in three days. (John 2:19)

Q: According to Jesus, what must we do to see the kingdom of God?

A: Be born again. (John 3:6)

Q: What part of his disciples' bodies did Jesus wash?

A: Their feet. (John 13:4–5)

Q: What did Jesus offer the Samaritan woman by the well?

A: Living water. (John 4:10)

folder games

Q: Why did the royal official and his family from Cana become believers in Jesus Christ?

A: Because Jesus healed the royal official's son. (John 4:46–53)

Q: What did Jesus promise the Father would send to his disciples after he was gone?

A: The Friend, the Holy Spirit. (John 14:26)

Q: One day five thousand people listening to Jesus became hungry. What did Jesus use to feed them all?

A: Five small loaves of bread and two small fish. (John 6:9-11)

Q: One evening the disciples were out in a boat on the Sea of Galilee without Jesus. How did Jesus join them in the boat?

A: Jesus walked on the water. (John 6:19)

Q: What plant did Jesus call himself?

A: A vine. (John 15:1)

Q: Jesus' friend Lazarus was very sick. When Jesus finally came to see him, Lazarus was already dead. What happened next?

A: Jesus raised Lazarus from the dead so that Lazarus was alive again! (John 11:43–44)

Q: Who led the soldiers, priests and Pharisees to Jesus so they could arrest him?

A: Judas, one of Jesus' 12 disciples. (John 18:2)

Q: Who denied knowing Jesus three times before the rooster crowed?

A: Peter. (John 18:17, 25, 27)

Q: How was Jesus killed?

A: He was hung on a cross and crucified. (John 19:18)

Q: What happened three days after Jesus died?

A: He rose again! Jesus is alive! (John 20:10–17)

biff or balance

Criss Cross Puzzle Toss

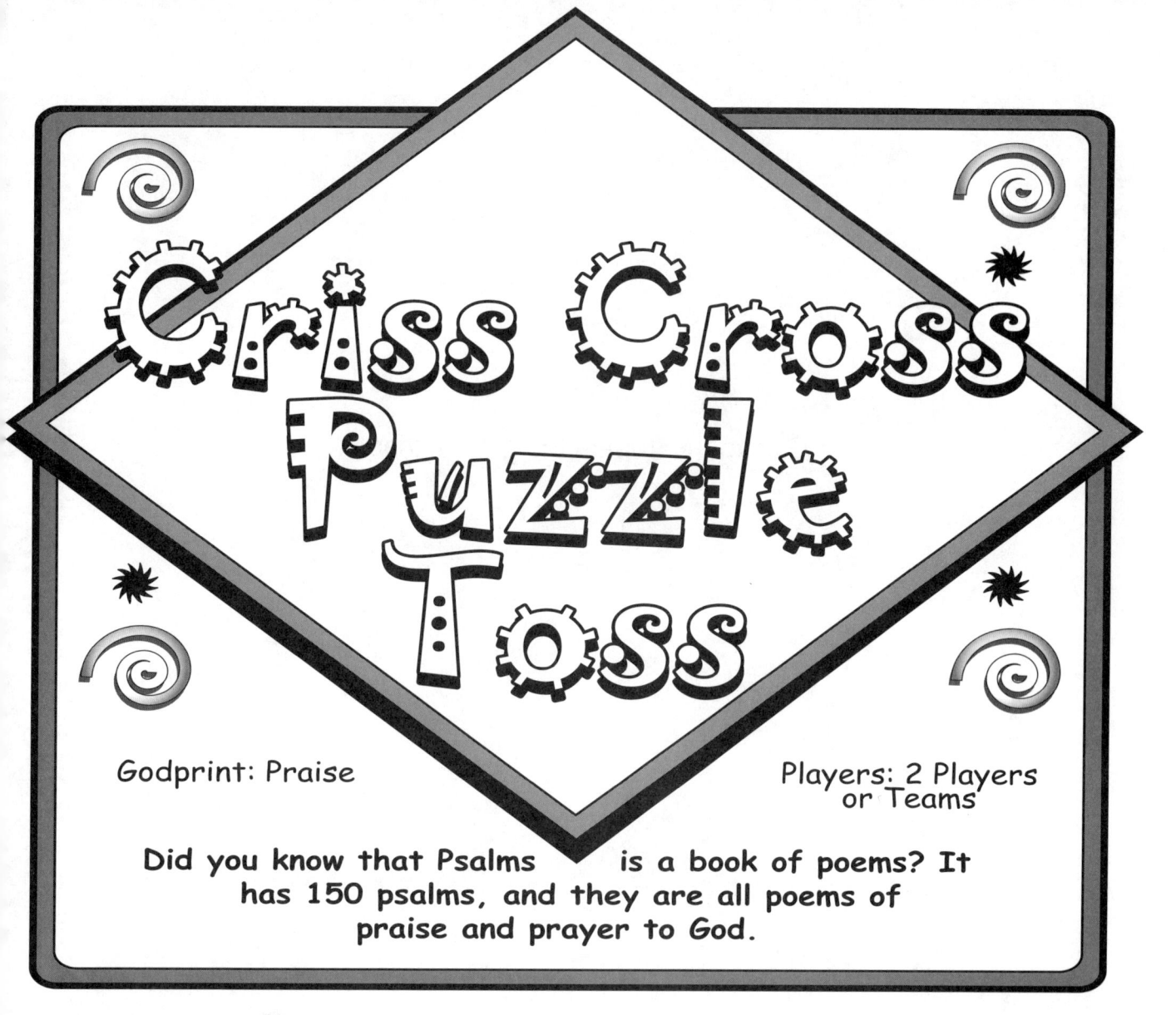

Godprint: Praise

Players: 2 Players or Teams

Did you know that Psalms is a book of poems? It has 150 psalms, and they are all poems of praise and prayer to God.

Put It Together

1. Glue the game title (above) to the front of a colorful file folder.

2. Tear out page 133, Poems of Praise and Prayer, and glue it the left inside of the game folder. Tear out the Criss Cross Gameboard, page 135, and glue it to the right side of your game folder. Hole punch the corners of the folder.

3. Now braid 24-inch lengths of yarn and crisscross the game folder from corner to corner. Knot in place and cut away the excess yarn. Make sure the folder can open to a right angle.

4. Tear out Psalm 23 (page 141), Psalm 100 (page 142) and Psalm 121 (page 143). Make two copies of each page. Follow the puzzle piece lines and cut each copy into 12 puzzle pieces. When you play the game, use only one psalm at a time.

5. Tear out the Puzzle Gameboards on pages 137 and 139.

6. Glue three zip-top bags to the back of the game folder, below How to Play. Label one bag for each psalm. Store the puzzle pieces here.

GET LIST:
- Bibles
- yarn
- hole punch
- 2 buttons
- 6 nine-ounce plastic cups
- game reproducibles
- 3 zip-top bags

Glue to the front of the game folder.

How to Play

GET LIST: ◆ 6 clear nine ounce plastic cups ◆ 2 buttons

1. The Psalms are full of praises of our great God and prayers to our loving God. Put the puzzles together and find out for yourself. The goal of this game is to collect all the puzzle pieces you need to make a psalm.

2. Choose Psalm 23, Psalm 100 or Psalm 121. Take the pieces out of the bag and mix them up.

3. Set the folder on the floor and prop it against a wall. Set six clear plastic cups on the circles. Put four psalm puzzle pieces in each of the six cups.

4. Stand about five feet away. Take turns throwing a button underhand into any of the cups. If the button misses a cup, it's the opposing team's turn. If the button lands in a cup, take your turn collecting a puzzle piece. (Fun variation: Make a rule that the buttons must hit the wall before dropping into cups.)

5. Pick out one of the puzzle pieces inside the cup your button landed in. Place it on the right spot of your puzzle gameboard. If you already have the piece, put it back in the cup. Maybe the other team needs it. Do not draw again. (Variation: If you pull out a piece you do not need, see if the other team does. Puzzle it over!)

6. The first team to have a complete puzzle of the psalm wins.

7. Play again with another psalm.

Cut out these playing rules and glue them to the back of the game folder.

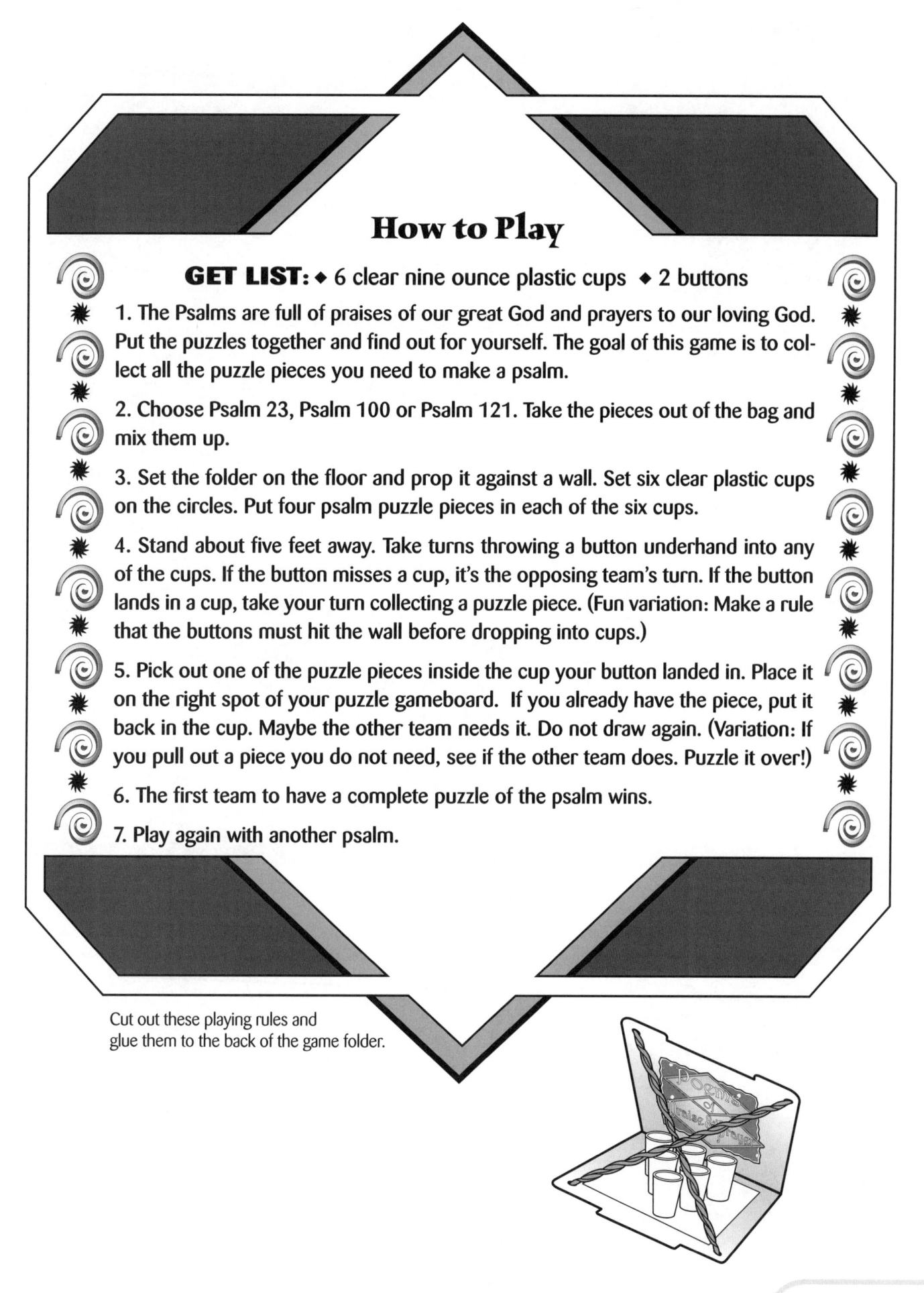

criss cross puzzle toss

Glue playing rules to the back of the game folder.

Glue to the left inside of the game folder.

Poems of Praise & Prayer

folder games

criss cross puzzle toss

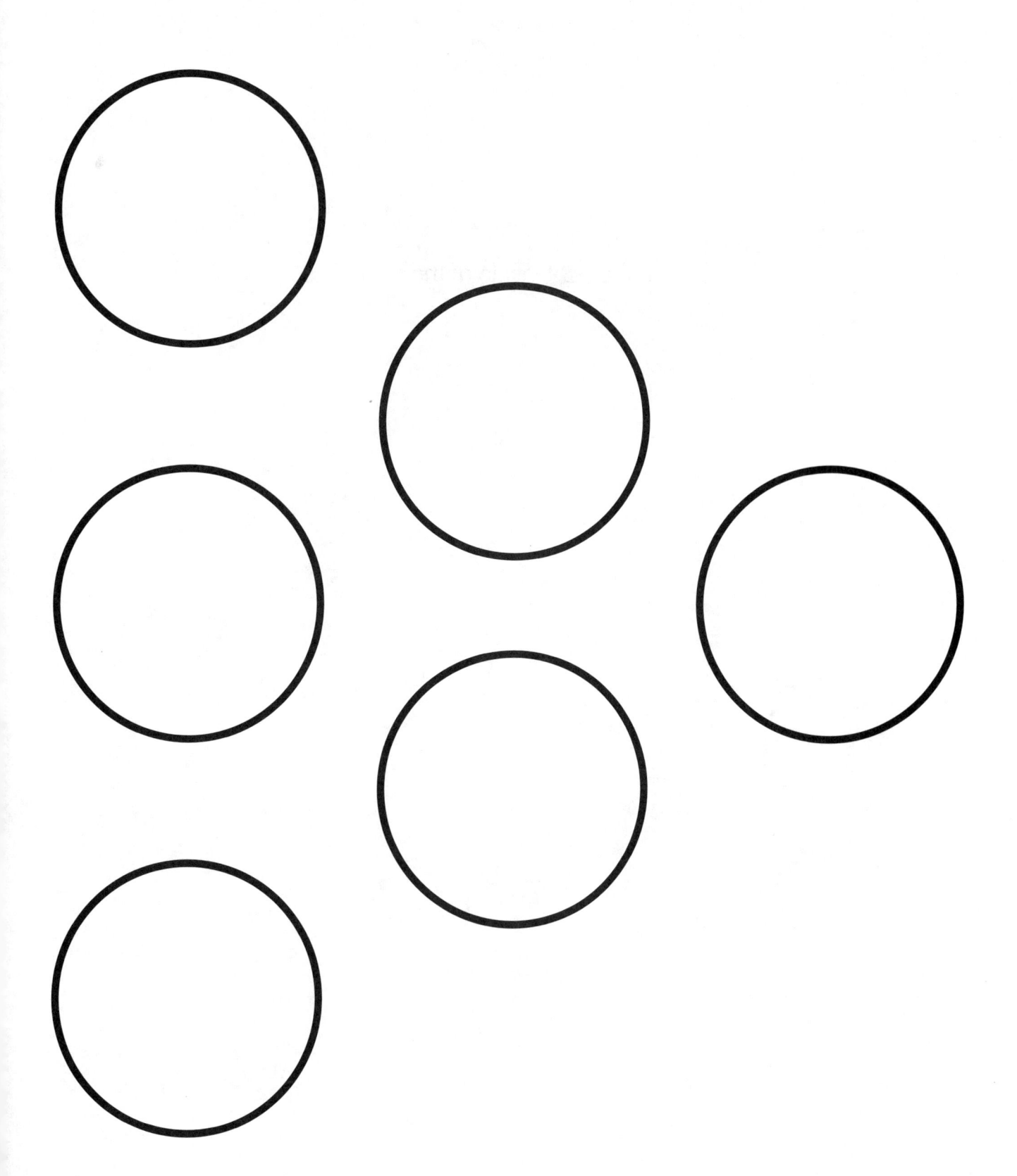

Glue to the right inside of the game folder.

criss cross puzzle toss

137

folder games

criss cross puzzle toss

folder games

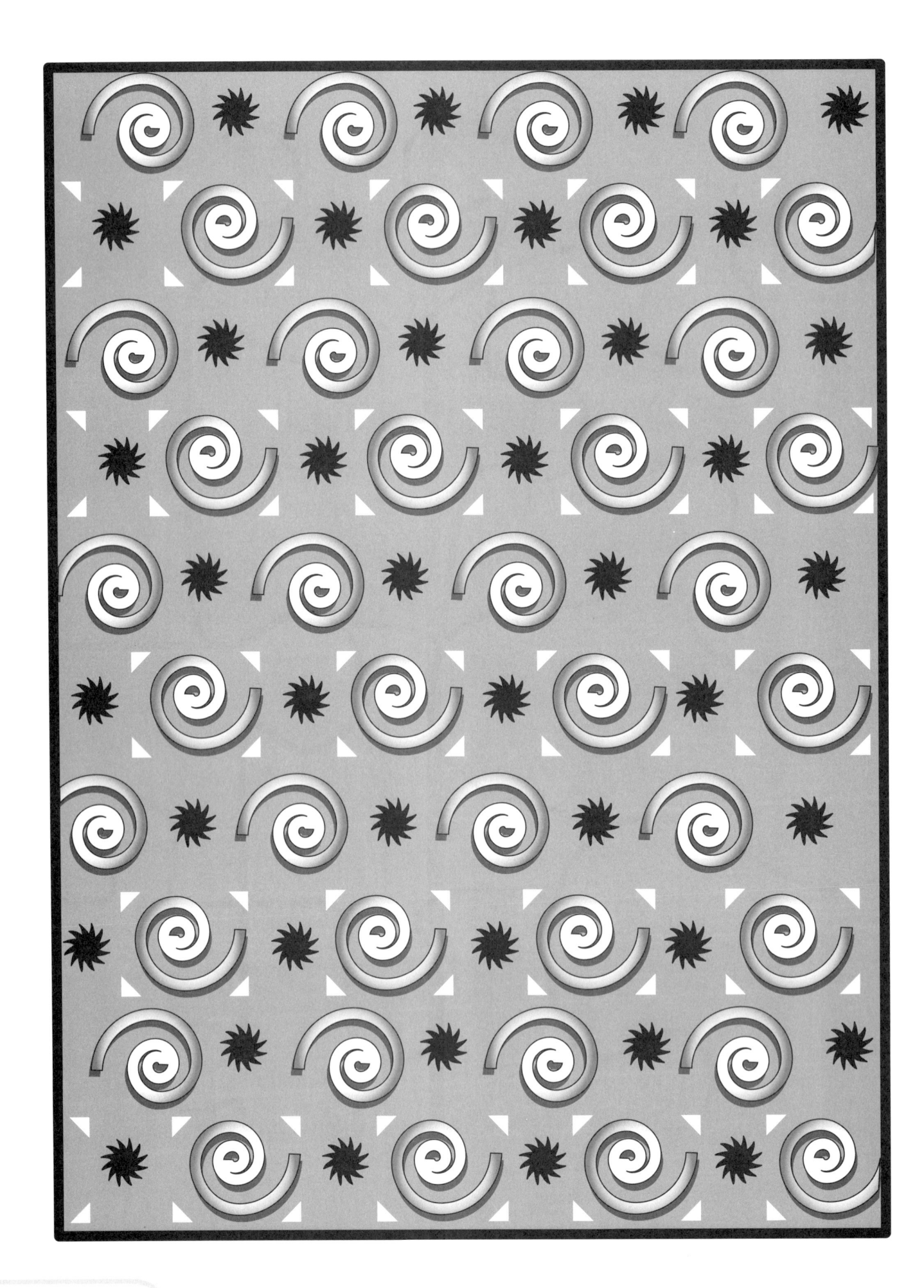

Psalm 23

The Lord is my shepherd,
I shall not be in want.
He makes me lie down in green pastures,
he leads me beside quiet waters,
he restores my soul.
He guides me in paths of righteousness
for his name's sake.
Even though I walk through the valley
of the shadow of death,
I will fear no evil, for you are with me;
your rod and your staff,
they comfort me.
You prepare a table before me in
the presence of my enemies.
You anoint my head with oil;
my cup overflows.
Surely goodness and love will follow me
all the days of my life, and I will dwell in
the house of the Lord forever.

©Copyright Cook Communications Ministries. Permission to reproduce.

criss cross puzzle toss

Psalm 100

Shout for joy to the Lord,
all the earth.
Worship the Lord with gladness;
come before him with songs of joy.
Know that the Lord is God.
It is he who made us, and we are his;
we are his people and
the sheep of his pasture.
Enter his gates with thanksgiving
and his courts with praise;
Give thanks to him and
praise his name.
For the Lord is good and
his love endures forever;
his faithfulness continues
through all generations.

©Copyright Cook Communications Ministries. Permission to reproduce.

Psalm 121

I lift up my eyes to the hills—
where does my help come from?
My help comes from the LORD,
the Maker of heaven and earth.
He will not let your foot slip—
he who watches over you will
not slumber; indeed, he who
watches over Israel will neither
slumber nor sleep. The LORD
watches over you—the LORD is
your shade at your right hand;
the sun will not harm you by day,
nor the moon by night. The LORD
will keep you from all harm—he
will watch over your life; the LORD
will watch over your coming and
going both now and for evermore.

Index

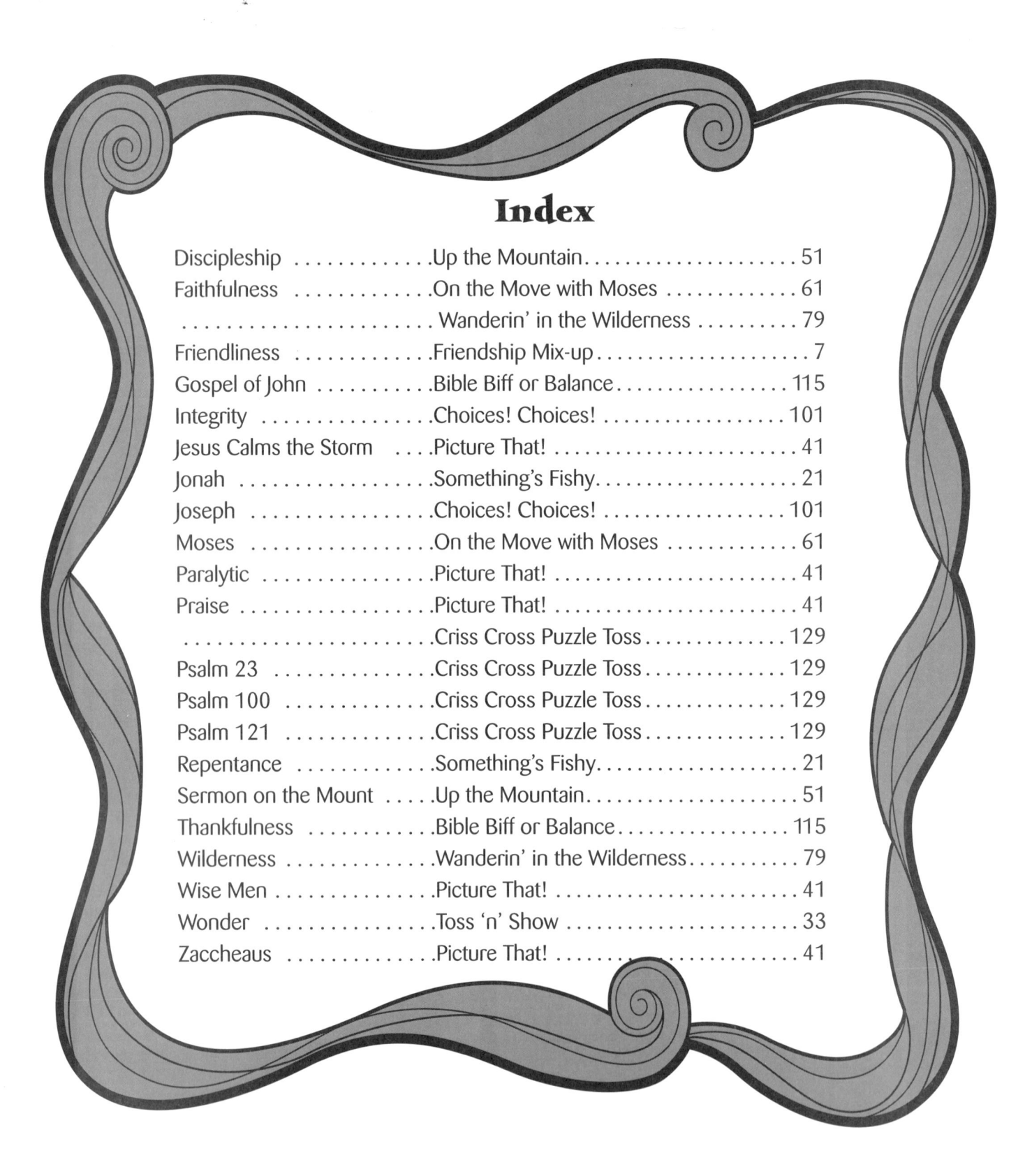

Discipleship	Up the Mountain	51
Faithfulness	On the Move with Moses	61
	Wanderin' in the Wilderness	79
Friendliness	Friendship Mix-up	7
Gospel of John	Bible Biff or Balance	115
Integrity	Choices! Choices!	101
Jesus Calms the Storm	Picture That!	41
Jonah	Something's Fishy	21
Joseph	Choices! Choices!	101
Moses	On the Move with Moses	61
Paralytic	Picture That!	41
Praise	Picture That!	41
	Criss Cross Puzzle Toss	129
Psalm 23	Criss Cross Puzzle Toss	129
Psalm 100	Criss Cross Puzzle Toss	129
Psalm 121	Criss Cross Puzzle Toss	129
Repentance	Something's Fishy	21
Sermon on the Mount	Up the Mountain	51
Thankfulness	Bible Biff or Balance	115
Wilderness	Wanderin' in the Wilderness	79
Wise Men	Picture That!	41
Wonder	Toss 'n' Show	33
Zaccheaus	Picture That!	41